THE DAYS OF MAWATANI

The Boy Who Turned Himself Around

CECILE OUELLET

Brilliant Books Literary
137 Forest Park Lane Thomasville
North Carolina 27360 USA

The Days of Mawatani should have great appeal to young fans of Ann Nolan Clark's Secret of the Andes and Scott O'Dell's many novels of indigenous American life. Like those authors, Ouellet provides an intense sense of history and level of anthropological detail without sacrificing emotional power or narrative flow. Ouellet makes a refreshing and unusual choice in focusing on only the Lakota way of life, rather than on indigenous-European clashes (though a brief mention of Lewis and Clark hints at such conflicts to come).

Mawatani is a sympathetic but thoroughly realistic character, one with whom middle school and older elementary school readers should have no trouble identifying. Both educational and engaging, Ouellet's novel would make a stimulating supplement to a school history curriculum.

BlueInk Heads Up: Highly recommended for young fans of Scott O'Dell, as well as for educators.

Blueink Review

I knew almost nothing about the Lakota culture when I began reading, and yet, within pages, I felt myself being transported back through time. The story of Mawatani envelopes the reader (of whatever age!); lessons of a life in harmony with nature so needed today are gently revealed. This is a story which remains in the heart and mind of the reader. What a pleasure!

Clair E. Villano – Educator

Ms. Ouellet has written a compelling narrative about a young Oglala boy between childhood and young adult. Her research comes through in the details of Plains Indians life, bringing vivid energy to the story. This book will appeal to youthful and adult readers interested in Native American culture.

Elizabeth Nelms – NCTM

Young people rejoice! You have a great read created just for you. Cecile Ouellet knows her audience and writes with passion, clarity, joy and inspiration.

Helen Cahill

I found the book The Days of Mawatani by Cecile Ouellet that it captivated my interests in Native American history this summer. Being part Choctaw Indian from Oklahoma I could understand the spirit of Mawatani an Indian boy trying to find himself on a personal level in his life struggles. I would like to see young American kids read this book at school and learn how the Native people look at themselves to see that we all are not so different. Cecile takes you to another time with this young Indian boy who struggles with life but he finds out the importance of family and friends along his journey. I would recommend this book for young people to enjoy reading and learning about Native people.

Enjoyable and intriguing read.

Diane Bircher

I thoroughly enjoyed reading "The Days of Mawatani" and send my hearty congratulations on beautiful story that is extremely well told. Your writing style is delightful, Cecile, and while this was written for a younger audience, I was thoroughly absorbed by the story as it unfolded, The Prologue was a "grabber" and peaked my attention to see how this young man's life unfolded after such a serious tragedy. This was a tender book with rich lessons, all shared through the culture of the Lakota. Brilliantly done and thoroughly enjoyed! I appreciate both your pronunciation guide and glossary – these facilitated a much more authentic understanding of the story. Brilliant additions!

Margie King – Former Chapman
University representative to Alumni

Many Native American cultures measure wealth by what an individual is willing to give away and not by the measure of one's possessions. Ms. Ouellet gives away her heart to the reader through the character of Mawatani. Her extensive research is impeccable. I loved this story and so did my grandchildren.

Donna JO McFadden

I became totally immersed in Cecile Ouellet's coming-of-age book about an Oglala Indian youth. The story flows smoothly through events and native locations graphically portraying the culture and language. The author has painstakingly studied Lakota words and phrases and uses them to add depth and authenticity throughout the book. The characters are dramatic and realistic. I believe that young adults will appreciate the book as well as older readers interested in other cultures.

Patricia Ann Reid- author

This is a must read for young adults. The story follows a boy thru trials of his life and cultural expectations.The reader becomes Mawatani and asks the question, What would I do? He reaches the right path. Memorable book.

-Nina Rockley

Dedicated to Red Cloud Indian School where
great things are happening in education

Contents

Part IV — The Preparation

Part V — Hanbleceya

Acknowledgements

Having a book published is an exciting personal event, though it would not have happened without the support of others. There were many librarians who, I'm sure, began to say, "Oh Lord, here she is again," and friends who probably thought "Will you shut up about the book, already!" This is all assumption, of course, because this book would not exist if it was not for the support I received from many people.

My technical support came from three states. Thanks go to Dave and Sandra Henry (Colorado), who were always there when the computer began to misbehave, and to Jan Bolton (California), who attempted to save my sanity when the computer boldly teased me with various and sundry glitches. As to the sanity part--- that is still to be determined. Then there's Dru Hanich (Wyoming), who saved the day when my computer refused to allow me to send my manuscript. With grit, and determination she solved the problem. Other thanks go to my cousin, Dian Jackson, who encouraged me from the start and is the foundation of this second publication. Many thanks to my friend, Donna who supported me in many ways, and a pilyama (thanks) to Ken Little, (Dakota)who helped me with the Lakota language. Big hugs to Naomi Nedleman, Ronnie Reader, and Lorna Bryant for their editing support. A very appreciative thanks to Tina Merdanian, from Red Cloud Indian School, who was so helpful in getting permission to use the revised-to-fit-the-story, Indian prayer.

Pilyama (Thank you)

Preface

The story of this book has been ruminating for years. I began to write it in the 1980's, but life kept getting in the way of completing it. Hours were spent in libraries, museums, and engrossed in books at my home. I had the opportunity to speak with two Oglala acquaintance and a Dakota friend. I was even allowed to speak with Tom Little, grandson of Sitting Bull, before he died. Putting all this information together, I discovered many variances of opinions in regard to customs and ceremonies. This left me having to pick and choose the information that was, hopefully, the most accurate. Accuracy was an important goal for this work, and I sincerely hope the result shows my deep respect for the Lakota and all indigenous peoples.

Note: though Mawatani is introduced as an Oglala, you will see mentioned, throughout, both Lakota and Sioux. The Sioux Nation, called The Seven Council Fires, includes seven, closely related tribes. The Lakotas are a subtribe of the Teton Sioux. The Oglala are a band of the Lakota. This is actually, a wonderfully interesting study. Check it out sometime. You might be amazed by the scope of the people called the Sioux.

Pronunciation Guide for Names

Mawatani (Ma<u>wa</u>tani)	young Oglala boy
Steals Many Horses	Mawatani's father
Holy Moon Woman	Mawatani's mother
Capa Win<u>ha</u>ha (Chapa Win<u>ha</u>ha)	Mawatani's younger brother
Comes Alone	Mawatani's baby brother
Takcawe (Tahk<u>cha</u>way)	Mawatani's sister
Bear Walker	Mawatani's Uncle
Talks With Owls	A Wakan Wicasa (holy man)
Catches Tail	Mawatani's cousin
Six Toes	Mawatani's friend
Matoska (Ma<u>tosh</u>ka	Mawatani's teenage friend
Etonka (Ee<u>ton</u>ka)	nickname for Matoska
Night Eagle	chief of neighboring village
Hears The Voice	medicine man of neigbnoring village
Walls in Silence	medicine man of neighboring village
Singing Lark	wife of Night Eagle
Zicahota (Zi<u>cha</u>hota)	Mawatani's friend from neighboring village
Kimimila (Ki<u>mi</u>mila)	Zicahota's sister
Cankuwaste (Chan<u>ku</u>washtay)	medicine man
Napasne (Na<u>paysh</u>nee)	Mawatani's horse

Prologue

The Tale Begins

Dwarfed by the expansive plains, an Oglala brave and his young son, Mawatani, strolled casually toward the Northeast. Each carried a combination quiver and bow case over his shoulder. A domesticated wolf walked beside them, pulling a small travois, a carrier made from two poles attached to his body. It held supplies and their buffalo robes.

Their day began on the prayer mountain near their village. Steals Many Horses thanked Wakan Tanka, the Great Spirit, and Tunkasila, the Grandfather Creator, for giving them life. The prayer ended with a plea for a safe journey.

No horses would be used this trip. There was no hurry. This was a time of leisurely ambling across the plains, taking in all that Grandmother Earth had provided them. The only reason they brought the wolf was to carry their heavy robes needed during the cold nights and early mornings.

Mawatani was excited. This was a mentoring trip. All young Oglala boys had mentors. For him, it was his Uncle, Bear Walker. Most mentors were uncles. Once in a while, Steals Many Horses liked to take his son out to let him show what he learned.

Mawatani always enjoyed the trips with his Uncle, but the few he took with his Father were special. He had seen twelve winters now and looked forward

Cecile Ouellet

to this father and son trip before the Spring buffalo hunt. What he enjoyed most was their time together. He was especially pleased when he found out they were going to one of his favorite places. There were many rabbits there at this time of year. He loved the luscious aroma of the roasting rabbit. It smelled as good as it tasted.

This was the fifth Spring Mawatani and his father had taken a mentoring trip. This day they were setting out for an area just South of Cedar Butte, near the confluence of the White River and the Cankpte Opi Wakpala, the creek known as Wounded Knee.

The trip was going to takea little longer this year. Their tiyospaye, a close-knit extended family community, usually settled North of this year's encampment. After the last buffalo hunt they settled South on Blacktail Creek, West of the White River.

They spoke of many things as they walked. Steals Many Horses mentioned he was watching when Mawatani won the "hoop and pole" game the day before.

"There were many young men playing with you... koskalakas, two or three years older than you," he said. "Matoska, especially, was not happy with you. He is almost two years older than you and could not keep up."

"Matoska is never happy about anything anymore," Mawatani answered. "We don't even call him Matoska anymore. We call him Etonka now because he never stops talking and he complains about everything."

"I can't see how he could complain about the way you played," his Father said. "You do not play like a young boy anymore. hoksilas your age do not play with such skill. You are even getting too good for me to play you this game. It would be embarrassing to have a son score more than his até. On the other

2

hand, my pride in you would probably make up for my embarrassment. A Father takes pride in these thing, you know." He gave Mawatani a fatherly cuff on the shoulder.

"Pilamaya. Thank you, Até. I work hard at playing well."

"That is quite obvious, my son."

"Até, sometimes I think Matoska hates me. Every time I am with my friends he tries to make trouble. He is no longer fun to be with."

"I believe he is jealous of you. When you and your friends were younger, you looked to him for leadership. Now, they look to you. He will outgrow this. Matoska is a koskalaka now; a young man. He should not be spending his time with the young hokshilas. He has not yet accomplished his first hanbleceya, his first vision quest. Twice he has gone to the mountain for a vision, but none have come to him. He needs to spend more time learning the stories to help him prepare for his next quest."

The cool, crisp morning had blossomed into one of those early Spring days that hints of the summer to come. Anpetu wi, the sun, had not even reached halfway to the middle of the sky when it became too warm for the heavy robes. This Spring was milder than usual.

Looking West, the dark peaks of the Black Hills interrupted the plains with its sharp and rambling contours. Known as the Paha Sapa, these beautiful hills had been sacred to those who lived there since time began.

Finding an area with an abundance of various plants, Steals Many Horses asked Mawatani to tell him about them.

Without hesitation, the boy explained each one, describing its use and how it helped or hurt their

3

people. He told which were used for food, for healing and what they healed. He pointed out which were used for dyes or paints, and how some of them had multiple uses.

"Well done, my son. Bear Walker has taught you well."

As they continued walking East, up ahead, well defined by the morning sun, was the Makosica, the Badlands. They spread bizarre shadows to the Wet, and extraordinary beauty across the plains.

These banded mountains, with strange, jagged spires, rose from the Earth as though the spirits had grown tired and thrown leftovers from the Paha Sapa to the ground. The discarded remnants remained where they landed.

The Lakota call these plains the otankaya toyola, the extended green. To the West, as far as the eyes could see, is a carpeted dirt, a rocky, but grassy carpet covered the flatlands and the hilly plains.

To the South stood the rugged hills they had crossed earlier. They walked in silence for a while, then Steals Many Horses called out, "Mawatani, look ahead," He pointed upstream. "Over there, do you see? It is the tree we planted the first year we were here together."

The boy spotted the tree and was amazed. "Look how it has grown, Até. Grandmother has fed it well."

Mawatani ran up a small rise for a better look. His slim body was muscular for his age; his movements agile and expressive. He was a handsome boy with eyes set apart by a sculptured nose, framed above by thick eyebrows. Heavy lashes accented his deeply set dark brown eyes. Self-confidence flowed from him. His smile always began in his eyes, which brightened, and appeared to dance before his lips took the clue and turned upward into the smile.

Looking in all directions, they took in the beauty of the land. Spring on the prairie was always a special gift from Grandmother Earth. Emerging from the short grasses were prairie violets, blue hooded phlox, and other Spring blossoms. Their colors of blue, red and yellow brightened the landscape. Purple vetch entwined itself around anything that grew in its way.

Steals Many Horses took this opportunity to quiz Mawatani about all they saw. Again, he showed his knowledge of the plant life and all it had to offer.

"Até, is the land not beautiful?"

"Yes, it is beautiful," his father answered. "Grandmother is good to us."

The talk turned to the upcoming buffalo hunt and how nice it will be to have fresh meat from tatanka, the sacred buffalo.

After a few moments, Mawatani made an announcement.

"I am not going to ride with the hokshilas and chase calves. This year I will bring in my own buffalo."

"That is not an easy task, Mawatani. It is difficult to penetrate the hide of a grown buffalo. It is not like sending an arrow to a calf."

"I understand that, Até, but I can do it. I am sure of it."

"You have had little experience with a buffalo horse. I don't know, Mawatani. We will see," his father replied. "Perhaps you are right."

Mawatani loved to hear the story of the capture and kidnapping of his father. He coaxed him into telling it again.

"It was many moons ago, when I was only four winters old," Steals Many Horses began. "A brave from our Mandan tiyospe killed a koskalaka from your mother's tiyospe. Tall Tree, a chief from her village, came to seek revenge, bringing several braves. I

5

was frightened and hid in a bush. Tall Tree saw me hiding and picked me up. He and his braves rode off with me and returned to their home. They called me Hides In Bush for many years. Tall tree adopted me and treated me like a son. He was a good até."

"Tell me about when you changed your name. That is a good story."

"You have heard it many times, Mawatani."

"I know, Até, but it is such a good story. Please?"

"Very well. Our tiyospe had few horses," Steals Many Horses began. "Soon after my first hanbleceya, I asked two of my friends to join me in raiding a Crow village. We were so quiet, not one person heard us until we released all of their horses. The sleeping villagers did not know what happened until it was too late. Twenty-six horses were captured. It was then when they began to call me Steals Many Horses."

Mawatani was proud of his até and looked up to him. He was one of the most respected man of the tiyospe. *The Great Spirit did me honor by making me his son,* he thought. *I will be a great warrior like him when I am grown.*

Occasionally, they would stop and sit, not just to rest, but to become one with Grandmother Earth. She was pleased when they joined her in spirit.

Mawatani watched as lizards slithered across sun-warmed rocks. Prairie dogs peeked from their burrows and chatted, while others stood at attention, serving as sentries against possible danger.

Steals Many Horses chanted prayers of thanks for Mitakuye Oyasin, all our relations. These included all the earth people; the two-leggeds, the four-leggeds and the winged people, plus fire, rock, water, and all things that grow.

The two sat, enjoying the rest. Even the wolf joined in, sharing his pleasure of life by enthusiastically wagging his tail and licking Mawatani on the face.

Mawatani looked to the North at the chaotic outline of the Macosica. Smiling, he thought *it looks like a large, mysterious village where giant people live in high and ragged tipis without poles. Grandmother earth must have a sense of humor to have placed this large mass of rock and dirt in the middle of the otankaya toyola.*

Hearing a noise nearby, Mawatani and his father watched as two young ferrets scampered around a bush. "Look, Até. They are fun to watch. They move so quickly and change directions so fast it seems impossible."

"Yes, they have charm and are fun to watch," his Father answered, "but look over there, by the bush. I doubt that bull snake sees their charm."

Mawatani looked and saw the snake looking at two of her eggs. They were broken and the contents eaten by the rambunctious rodents.

"It is all a part of the circle of life, Mawatani. The two-leggeds, the four-leggeds and the winged people keep balance in this life. It is Grandmother's plan."

They spoke about the two braves from the Miniconjous village who came to their tiyospaye a few days earlier. The visitors told them about many white men from the East who traveled on the River of the Muddy Waters. The white man called the river the Missouri and said the men were being led by two men called Lewis and Clark. They were going far away where the great river meets a giant ocean. The braves did not know this word ocean, but were told it was like a giant lake that took over the Earth. This made them wonder if this could mean more white men were coming.

Mawatani asked his Father to retell the story of the night when he was born, when hanhepi wi, the night sun disappeared.

"The night was bright with hanhepi wi when they took your mother to the birthing lodge," Steals Many Horses began. "As her pain increased, a shadow began to cover its light, and soon, hanhepi wi disappeared. We had seen this happen before, but it still caused alarm among our people.

"Just as the light began to show, like the curve of a drawn bow, we heard your first cry. As you entered the world, hanhepi wi was reborn, and sent its light down to us. At first, we called you Boy Who Came With Moon. As you grew, we named you Mawatani. It was then, too, that we began to call your mother Holy Moon Woman. Before, she was called Zanta Ohinni, because she was always faithful and trustworthy."

Their walk continued with a mix of conversation and quiet. As afternoon approached, clouds began to form over the Paha Sapa. By the time they reached their destination within a copse of trees, hanhepi, the night, was near. The skies were turning dark and a pale hanhepi wi peeked in and out of the clouds. Sounds of the Thunderbeings grew closer.

Rushing into the sparse protection of the trees, the two began to set up camp. While Steals Many Horses prepared a fire, Mawatani searched for material to use as fuel.

Suddenly, a streak of lightning flashed from the skies, striking a nearby tree with such force, it split in two. The bolt completed it destructive journey by striking the chest of Steals Many Horses, continuing through his body and into the wolf standing next to him.

At the deafening clap of thunder, Mawatani turned and saw his father lying near the campsite.

"Até mi tawa...my Father!" Mawatani cried out. He ran to help, but his run was cut short. The falling half of the dissected tree slammed into his leg, forcing him to the ground and knocking him unconscious. His right leg was mangled. Bone protruded through his flesh, and his blood reddened the earthen floor.

The scene, so peaceful a few seconds earlier, had turned to disaster. Steals Many Horses had laid down his robe, and was now entering the Land of Many Lodges, for he was dead.

Mawatani was unconscious, trapped, and seriously injured. In the time spent to take a breath, his life was changed forever.

The rabbits would be safe tonight.

PART I
THE IMPASSE

Chapter 1

. . . .

Wacinco—One Who Feels
Sorry For Himself

Rain pounded the Lakota village along Willow Creek, where the tiyospaye had settled after the spring buffalo hunt. The rain had been relentless for the past three days, saturating the land. Small puddles joined with others, forming great pools within the circle of dwellings. Outside, dogs lay close to their masters' lodges; many begging to enter. Some got their way.

The downpour brought more water than the people had ever seen during a single storm. What began as a few showers on their return from the buffalo hunt, turned into an intense deluge; a relentless cloudburst showing no signs of ending. As a result, the creek was nearing its crest. The headmen, who were responsible for order in the village, warned the people to be ready to move out if it did not stop soon.

Many new hides for tipis still needed to be prepared and sewn together. Some of the older hides in use were worn and did not serve well in this weather. Day was barely discernible from night. In this early morning, through the drenching rain, fires within the tipis sent an eerie glow throughout the camp; like an apparition; a village of spirit dwellings.

Inside one lodge, the fire spread warmth and light to the wet, cold, dark day. Holy Moon Woman knelt by a buffalo paunch cooking pot, in which she had placed water, fresh buffalo meat, wild turnips, and onions. She added maize and her favorite herbs for the finishing touch. The stones on the fire were now hot enough to place in the pot. Soon the aroma of today's soup would fill the air. Many said that hers was the best soup in the village.

Yawning, with sleepy eyes only half open, a mongrel dog lay inside the entrance, staring at the antics of two boys.

Comes Alone, a baby wrapped in buffalo fur, squirmed in his cozy cradleboard. It stood tied with a thong to one of the poles that framed the tipi. It was good that the board was tied securely. The baby was squirming in giggles, delighted by the teasing of Capa Winhaha, his fun-loving older brother, who was almost five.

Takcaway, their nine-year-old sister, sat on her willow bed mat mending a worn parfleche, a rawhide pouch used for carrying and storing. She was humming a tune of her own making.

A 13-year-old boy sat on his bed mat, staring into space. In his hand he held a bone needle, threaded with sinew. A small parfleche lay across his lap.

"Mawatani," his mother said, "do not just sit there. You must do what you can."

The boy looked at his sister as she mended. *I have become a woman*, he thought. *Boys do not mend*.

A year had passed since Steals Many Horses died. Mawatani spent much of his time reliving that day. He could not forget the terror and pain that left him fatherless and crippled, with a right leg that was beyond repair.

Mawatani's tiyospaye and the neighboring one that helped him, often joined during the buffalo hunts. He vaguely knew who they were, but he was unable to erase from his mind the confusion he felt when he awoke to find himself in a strange village with people he really did not know. He was being cared for by their medicine men when he was told his father was dead. Their words echoed in his mind.

Now, he thought, *I am crippled, never to become a great warrior as my até was. It would be better to die than to spend the rest of my life doing nothing but the work of a woman.*

There were times when he was grateful to those people from the neighboring village who found him, treated his wounds, and returned him to his family. Most of the time, however, he wished they had just left him by his father to die. This was one of those times.

Sitting motionless in thought, Mawatani stared at his surroundings. To the left of the entry, three parfleches hung on the wall next to a willow-rod backrest. A larger parfleche lay on the floor beneath them. Three other bed mats lay nearby. Six had lived there before the last buffalo hunt, but Holy Moon Woman's mother died on their way to the new camp. Mawatani's mother's hair was short again. She cut it when her mother died, as she did when his father was killed.

It seemed strange now, without an old one living there. He missed his unci, his grandmother, who had lived with them since he was a small boy. Now, there was no old one to live with them.

Mawatani watched Capa Winhaha as he played with Comes Alone, the little one he loved, yet resented. The baby did not fill the void left by the loss of his até, who never even knew he was to be a

15

father again. Even if the baby's twin had lived, the empty place of Steals Many Horses would not have been filled. The second baby died as it was born, to begin its life as a spirit, perhaps to be born again.

On the wall opposite the entrance, Steals Many Horses' bow and quiver hung next to his shield. Usually, these would have been placed with his body for use in the next world, but his body was never recovered. The two men who came upon the tragic scene saw that Mawatani was still alive and took him to their village. By the time they returned for Steals Many Horses, his body was gone, probably dragged off by some four-legged to use as sustenance for its own life. The men retrieved his bow and quiver and returned them along with Mawatani.

Again, Holy Moon Woman scolded her son.

Mawatani's teeth clenched in anger and his eyes squinted in defiance. He threw the parfleche to the ground, turned away from his mother and said aloud, but to himself, "I am not a woman. I do not mend!" He wanted so much to shout this directly to her face, but a boy his age never spoke directly to his mother. It just wasn't done.

Seldom did a young man of the Sioux raise his voice in anger at home. Children of the plains always learned patience, understanding, and acceptance of circumstances when it came to home life. That was the only way a tiyospaye could survive.

Mawatani did not understand his own behavior. He knew it confused and saddened his mother and siblings. His friends were also confused, and a few called him wacinko, which means boy who feels sorry for himself.

Everyone wants me to be who I used to be, he thought. *They wants me to be the boy who always obeys, leads his peers, and wins every game and race. That person no longer exists. They will have to accept that. I have a right to feel sorry for myself.*

Mawatani's Uncle, Bear Walker, who was now his father, often spoke about his behavior with Talks with Owls, a Wicasa Wakan; a wise and holy man. The old man's spiritual medicine was respected throughout the Sioux nation. Twice, he and Bear Walker entered the initi, the sweat lodge, for that was the only way to become purified and gain understanding. They shared the cannunpa, the sacred pipe, in prayer, asking the Great Spirit for guidance. So far, they had received no answers.

The problem was not only that Mawatani refused to contribute his share within the tiyospaye. His attitude was beginning to impact the whole village, which was especially harmful to the younger children. Something had to be done.

Chapter 2

· ·

The Challenge

The rain finally began to subside, and within a few days, the waters of the swollen creek flowed powerfully within its banks. Anpetu wi, the sun, appeared and began to evaporate the excess moisture of the land. Children who had been confined indoors, burst from their lodges and spent their pen-up energy in muddy games.

Mawatani sat on a rock near the creek watching the bustling activity of his village, but not really seeing. His thoughts were on the past, but this time, the recent past. He was pondering a dream of the night before.

Why do I continue to dream of the WAKINYAN, the Thunderbeings? I don't like these dreams, and I have had them all my life.

Dreams and visions were important to the Lakota. Mawatani was taught that dreams were messages from the spirits, meant to guide the dreamer toward his intended path in life. He did not like this path.

Dreams of the WAKINYAN often led to becoming a heyoka, a contrary. These were men who washed with dirt and dried in water. When they said yes, it meant no, and no meant yes. They even rode their horses facing the rear. Heyokas were good warriors and brought laughter and fun to the village, but he couldn't imagine having to learn to live life like that. It didn't feel right, so he told no one about these dreams.

Last night, though, it wasn't just thunder and lightning that entered his dreams. Last night's dream, as many of his dreams of the past, included a sungmanitu, the sacred wolf. He was not sure what that meant.

Only last year I was looking forward to my first hanbleceya, my first vision quest, he thought. *I hoped that the Great Spirit would send me a powerful vision to explain my dreams. Now, I no longer wonder about their meaning. I know what the dreams mean. The ones of lightning and thunder before my até was killed were forewarnings of things to come. The Thunderbeings were just forecasting that horrible day when the life I was to live, ended and my Father died. Those since, are no more than constant reminders of that tragic day.*

Dreams and visions are not good as I have been taught. They are only there to taunt me; to let me know things I don't want to know. Then they remind me of things I don't want to remember.

Etonka, a lanky young man, swaggered toward Mawatani. A few younger boys followed his lead. He looked down at Mawatani with contempt.

"Hey, wacinko, what's the matter? Does the poor little hoksila have nothing to do but sit and feel sorry for himself? Why aren't you with the rest of the women, gossiping and sewing?"

Mawatani looked away. *Ignore him; he is not here,* he thought.

Turning to the group of boys, Etonka said, "Look at him. He is a pitiful excuse for a hoksila old enough to be a koskolaka. You see, he is not man enough to look at me. He is even afraid to live his life. Uwau wo! Come with me," he said to the boys following. "We will not waste our time on him."

Most boys would not accept Etonka and let him know that they would not follow him. They still considered themselves friends of Mawatani and did not like the way he was being treated. They often wondered though, if Mawatani would ever be their friend again; if he would ever lead them again.

This did not keep Etonka from assuming leadership, especially with the youngest boys, who did not know Mawatani well. One thing he insisted these young boys do; call him by his real name, Matoska. White Bear is a good name.

Two of Mawatani's best friends, Six Toes and Catches Tail, who was Bear Walker's son, approached Etonka and took him aside. They let him know, in no uncertain terms, there would be no more negative talk about Mawatani.

"You tell him he is useless and acts like a child," Chases Tail said to him. "Look at you! You are two years older than he is and all you do with your life is try to lead small children. Your bad attitude is hurting them."

"How would you feel if you were suddenly in his place?" Six Toes asked. "Stay away from Mawatani. Leave these young ones alone. Go work on your own life with the koskalakas where you belong."

Etonka was obviously shocked by this tongue-lashing. A bit of moisture seemed to seep from his eyes as he turned and walked away.

That afternoon, Mawatani saw Bear Walker watching him. His Uncle approached him.

"Mawatani, it saddens me to see you like this. The people of our tiyospaye have great hopes for you. You have always been a natural leader. Your approach to life used to be full of enthusiasm and spirituality."

"Well, it is no longer, Uncle. How can I lead? I can barely walk."

Sadness and worry showed on the broad, weathered face of Bear Walker. He turned to look at the activity in the village. After a moment, he turned to his nephew and announced:

"Mawatani, tomorrow morning, before anpetu wi wakes, you and I will set out to the area where your father was killed, and you can hunt for rabbits."

"I cannot hunt," Mawatani said in disbelief. "I am crippled." He did not even look at his Uncle.

"You are not crippled," Bear Walker said. "You have one leg that is lame."

"I am crippled!" the boy repeated in defiance. "Besides, I do not want to go back into the trees."

Bear Walker shook his head. In a soft and patient voice, he replied, "A brave is not afraid of trees."

"I am not a brave," Mawatani cried out. "I will never be a brave. A brave can run and jump on his horse and leap over rocks. Even Takcawé can do that. I can't do those things. I am good only for mending."

Bear Walker's eyes flashed with anger. "You mean you will not do any of those things. You won't even try." He turned and walked away saying, "We will leave before sunrise tomorrow."

"We will take horses then," Mawatani shouted to his Uncle's back.

Bear Walker continued toward his lodge. "We will take no horses. We will travel as you did with your father."

"Ktesni. I will not go!" Mawatani yelled.

"You will go, Mawatani," Bear Walker said quietly. "You will go."

21

Chapter 3

• •

The Journey Begins

Holy Moon Woman and her children were sleeping soundly when Bear Walker entered their lodge and silently made his way to his nephew.

"Kiktawo, Mawatani," he whispered, "Wake up."

The boy yawned and turned over.

"No time for more sleep, Mawatani. Get up. Anpo Wicahpi, the morning star, is beginning to fade."

"Wa'u. I'm coming." Mawatani bristled as he stretched and yawned again. He rubbed his right leg, attempting to bring life to it. It took much longer for it to wake than the rest of his body. It was particularly a problem in the cold weather. The Moon When Ponies Shed had not yet come, and the night had been cold. Spring was much colder this year than last.

Slowly, he stood. His balance was never good when he first got up. He shivered as he put on a third shirt and his high, heavy moccasins while watching his uncle rekindle the fire. The tipi would be warm when his family woke.

Kneeling by his bed pad, he picked up a small parfleche packed with a digging knife and some pemmican. He placed a small container of ointment made from the ceyaka and icahpehu plants for when his leg began to ache and swell. Reaching for a more substantial knife, for skinning the rabbit or for protection, he paused, then changed his mind. *Bear Walker will have his knife. There is nothing I can do to protect anyone.* He placed the parfleche over his belt.

As Bear Walker rose from the fire and walked toward the entrance, he stumbled on two straight branches that Mawatani had prepared as a travois for the dog to pull.

"We will not take the dog today," Bear Walker whispered.

"Not take him? Then you will have to carry my bundles."

"The days are still cold," his uncle replied, "We will wear our robes. We won't need the dog to carry them. You will carry your own bundle," he added as he stepped outside.

"I can't carry them. Remember, I am crippled," Mawatani sarcastically added. He could not believe his Uncle was so pitiless. *He doesn't care that I am barely able to walk. How does he expect me to do this? My father would not be pleased that his brother is being so cruel to me, but Bear Walker is my father now. I must obey him.*

As he prepared his bed pad, he pictured it as his uncle, attempting to squeeze life from it as he rolled it up to carry. Using a leather strap to secure it, he placed it around the pad and tightened it, as if it was something he could strangle. He was not only angry at Bear Walker. His heart ached, believing that his uncle hated him. *He must hate me to treat me like this.*

After putting on his heavy buffalo robe, he placed his arm through the strap of the bedroll and hung it over his left shoulder. The extra weight almost caused him to fall. *Bear Walker will soon see I can't do this,* he thought, as he caught himself. *I am crippled. Why does no one understand this?*

As Bear Walker returned, Mawatani sneered and his whisper was sharp, curt and full of resentment. "I am ready, Até."

"That is good." Bear Walker glanced at Mawatani and asked, "Where are your bow and quiver?"

"You will have to shoot the rabbits. I can't," Mawatani answered.

Mawatani's defiance angered Bear Walker, and he motioned for them to leave the tipi. As they stepped outside, he spoke:

"Mawatani, since you were a small boy you have been taught never to leave the camp without your bow and quiver. Why do you now refuse?"

"I cannot use a bow. My body is too weak. Besides, I no longer have one."

"Your body is weak because your spirit is weak," Bear Walker snapped, "Where is your bow?"

"I burned it. I could no longer use it," Mawatani replied.

"Then you will take your father's bow and quiver," Bear Walker directed.

"Hiyesni! No! I will not take my father's bow. It is too large; too strong."

Bear Walker looked into Mawatani's eyes and gestured toward the tipi. Slowly and deliberately he said, "You will take your father's bow."

Mawatani's eyes flared and he began to challenge, but before he got the words out, his uncle spoke again, more softly and even slower.

"You will take your father's bow, Mawatani"

Breathing heavily, teeth clenched, lips tight in protest, Mawatani turned and entered his lodge. He stepped around his sleeping mother and lifted his father's quiver and bow case off of the wall. Attempting to place it on his shoulder, he discovered the bed roll was too bulky. The quiver would not stay. He removed the bed roll, ran his arm through the quiver strap and picked up the bed roll again. His balance was even worse now. His resentment grew.

How does Bear Walker expect me to make this long walk? I can barely stand. Clumsily, he made his way back to Bear Walker.

"Uncle, I cannot carry all this. I will fall."

Bear Walker saw the problem and placed another parfleche on the boy's empty shoulder. Among other things, it contained gifts for Eagle Eyes and his village. He decided it would be good to stop there on their way home to visit and catch up on any news.

"There," Bear Walker said, "this will even the weight and make it easier."

"Carry your own bundle," Mawatani said in defiance. "Wanma yanka yo! Look at me! I cannot even carry what I have." His anger was real. *No one seems to care that I am crippled. I am expected to carry on with my life as though nothing happened. It hurts.*

"It is good that you carry that bundle," Bear Walker said. "I have many other things to carry." He turned and began walking. "Uwo. Come, we must leave. We will begin on the paha wocekiye, the prayer mountain."

"Why don't you see that I cannot do this?" Mawatani cried out.

His uncle slowed his pace a bit but did not look back. "Why do you not see that you can?" Bear Walker asked quietly.

Mawatani began to follow in small, unsure steps, his right foot shuffling; dragging the ground. The dog followed, begging for attention. He received none.

Little by little, the boy's steps grew more confident. He had to admit that it was easier to walk now with the extra bundle than it had been before, but he wasn't going to let his uncle know that.

25

Bear Walker continued walking, slowing his usual pace, but not by much. He did not look back. His ears told him the boy was following.

The prayer mountain was barely a mountain at all. It was a hill with a gentle incline on one side. In contrast, the other side had collapsed, leaving scars down its sharp decline, as if some giant had scooped out a large bite, leaving only a protruding lip at the top. The result was a heavy out-cropping hanging over the steep flank.

Bear Walker directed the dog to stay and they began their climb. Even though the slope was gentle, Mawatani struggled to make headway. He zigzagged his way, sidestepping the muddy pools that stood in areas the sun had not reached. He could not keep his footing in the mud.

"Ama pe yanka, Uncle; wait for me. I need your help."

Bear Walker came back and offered his hand. Slowly, they reached the crest and made their way to the outcropping. This ledge served as an altar with a fire pit holding holy ashes from previous offerings. Round, sacred stones circled it.

Mawatani sat at the pit as his uncle started a small fire. When the flames grew steady, Bear Walker placed sage and sweetgrass on it, and soon the sacred smoke began to drift upwards, carrying its soothing perfume to their nostrils. Even Mawatani felt the holiness of the moment.

Bear Walker knelt close to the fire. With his hands cupped, he began to bring the smoke to his face, then directed it over and around his head and body. Soon its sacredness permeated his being, and he was one with the Great Spirit. This was to ward off the evil spirits and ask for the support of the good spirits.

Bear Walker looked at his nephew and gestured for him to do the same.

Mawatani paused. *Prayer is not much in my life any more, Uncle,* he thought. *My father and I began our last day together with prayer. Obviously, the Great Spirit was not doing much listening that day.* He decided it wasn't worth arguing over so, with little enthusiasm, he reached toward the smoke and directed it over his face.

They sat at the altar watching the coming of dawn. Anpo wi disappeared as light to the east began to set apart the dark morning sky from the prairie. Bear Walker stood, reached down to the boy's arm, and helped him stand.

When Mawatani rose, his uncle faced him, placing his hands on the boy's shoulders. Mawatani glanced into his uncle's eyes then quickly stared at the ground.

"Mawatani, you are my brother's son, and now, you are my son. I was outside the birthing lodge the night you were born; the night hanhepi wi, the moon, got lost. You left your mother's womb just as its light returned. The next morning, your father took you in his hands and raised you to the sky. He thanked the Great Spirit and dedicated you to Wakan Tanka, asking that you become the best you could be. That is what I want for you, Mawatani; to help you become the best man you can be. Do you understand?"

Mawatani kept his eyes to the ground. "I guess so."

"That is why I wanted to begin our journey here, on the prayer mountain. I will ask the Great Spirit to help us in this."

You pray all you want, Mawatani thought. *All I know is it didn't help my father much. He prayed, and a few hours later he was dead. And look what happened to me. I am crippled. Where was the Great Spirit that day?*

Looking down on their village and the swiftly flowing Willow Creek, Bear Walker stood in silence. He then turned to the East and raised his arms in prayer:

> * "Mitakuye oyasin...all my relations, hear me.
> O Tunkasila, Creator Grandfather, whose voice is heard in the winds, and who gives the world breath and life, let me walk the good red path in this life and make my eyes ever behold the beauty of the lands you have given us.
> Make our people respect the things you have made. Make our ears ready to hear your voice in the wind and all you have made. Let me learn the lessons you have hidden in every leaf and rock. Hear me! I need your strength and wisdom. I ask that you look with kindness and understanding upon this hoksila; this boy, who is my nephew; my son. Help him recapture his tawakan, his spirit, and see who he can be. Help him, find the good and brave spirit that dwells within him. Make us always ready to come to you with clean hands and straight eyes, so when life fades, as the fading sunset, our spirits may come to you without shame."

*This prayer is based on a Lakota prayer. Permission to adapt it to my story was given by Red Cloud Indian School, Inc.

Chapter 4

Moments of Remembering— Moments of Forgetting

The day passed quickly as uncle and nephew made their way along the west side of the White River. The river was running deep and swift. They would continue to follow this route to the North, where the river narrowed, before crossing.

Mawatani struggled, often losing his balance on the soggy, uneven ground. He often gazed at the Paha Sapa, the sacred Black Hills. Seeing the solidity of their rugged outline brought a sense of stability to his seemingly useless life.

After walking some distance, Mawatani began paying less attention to his lame leg. As he limped along, sometimes dragging his foot, he began to notice his surroundings and found himself joined in conversation with his uncle. They spoke of how the rain had brought the beginning of the taller grasses earlier than usual this year, and how the waters of the creek ran deeper and swifter than they had seen it before.

At a spot, near where the White River meets West Horse Creek, a beaver was shoring up an area of his dam that had been weakened from the pressure of the water's swift flow.

"Won't his dam stop the flow to our village?" Mawatani asked.

"No," answered Bear Walker. "You have seen the water coming into our camp. It is swift and high."

Bear Walker was pleased the boy asked this. Mawatani's spirit had been trapped within his wounded body for so long he had not spoken of such things.

"What if he builds his dam clear across the creek? Will that stop the flow?"

"No. The beaver is much wiser than that," answered his uncle. "The river is wide here. The beaver knows, if he blocked off the entire flow, the added pressure would destroy his lodge. We will have all the water we need." Bear Walker asked, "Why do you ask such a question? You learned the way of the beaver when you were just a small child."

"I guess I just haven't thought about these things for a while," Mawatani answered. "Yes, I do know about the beaver, and it was a silly question."

"I am pleased you talked about it, Mawatani," Bear Walker replied.

They reached the area where the White River began to narrow. Ahead, was the main crossing point at this part of the river. There was almost always a means of crossing here; sometimes a canoe; often a raft.

When they reached the crossing, a raft sat on shore. Mawatani was hesitant, but they crossed without incident and continued to the East.

Ahead, the plains were filled with the ripple and swells of the rolling hills. Mawatani continued to struggle. Going up these inclines was hard enough. Going down was even more difficult and painful. In spite of the difficulty, he remained surprisingly good-natured, pointing out the beauty of colorful flowers which were beginning to bloom.

Mawatani's leg was tiring, but he was actually enjoying himself. As they reached the top of a rise, he looked downstream and spotted the tree that he and his father planted. He made sure he was in back of his uncle, because tears began to form, and he did not want Bear Walker to see them.

Should I tell my Uncle about this tree? Mawatani thought. *No*, he decided. *This tree is special. It is a connection I still have with my ate.' I will not share this story now.*

As they drew closer to the Cankpe Opi Wakpala, the sounds of the heavy waters of the confluence of the creek with the White River began to be heard. Even though the White was well north of them, they could hear that the flow was more active than usual. Near the creek, much of the ground was still soft and muddy.

As they turned slightly North, to follow the creek, they could see smoke in the distance from the fires of Night Eagle's village. They were nearing their destination.

"We will catch extra rabbits and take them to Night Eagle before we return," Bear Walker said. "He likes rabbit too."

Their walk became silent as they neared the area of trees where Steals Many Horses was killed. Mawatani's memories were strong and painful.

Many miles were behind them when they stopped to make camp. It had been a long day. Mawatani was surprised he had been able to complete this long walk. Once he put his mind to it, he was even able to keep up most of the time. To his surprise, he enjoyed his uncle's company. It was not the same as

31

it was with his father, but there was good talk and good silence.

Dropping his bundles, Mawatani sat on a stump and closed his eyes. He was exhausted and his leg throbbed. He reached into his parfleche for ointment and applied some to his leg. *This day was good*, he thought. *I can't believe I made it.*

Bear Walker noticed a clearing across the creek. "We will stop and camp there, in that clearing," he said. "It is wide and level; a good place for our fire and for sleeping."

Mawatani's eyes widened and his mouth opened in a look of disbelief.

"I can't cross this creek. Look at it. I have never seen it run so swift and high. My leg will not carry me across the stones and branches. I'll fall and I can't swim."

"What do you mean, you can't swim. You could swim soon after you were born," Bear Walker countered. "Why do you think you can't cross the creek?"

In disbelief, anger and hurt, Mawatani shouted, "I was not crippled before. I will not try to cross it."

Bear Walker's voice remained calm. "No, of course you won't. You won't try much of anything anymore. Across the creek is the safest spot. That is where I will make camp. If you want to join me, you are welcome."

"You're going to leave me here alone?"

"I said you were welcome to join me," answered his uncle. "Then you must carry me across."

"I will not carry you. You can do this. You must try."

Taking the parfleche he had placed on Mawatani's shoulder, Bear Walker made his way across the creek.

Mawatani watched as his Uncle entered the water. "I will not even be able to make a fire", he said to Bear Walker. "You are taking the fire kit."

"I will make a good fire at my camp," Bear Walker said. "You must join me."

The boy, close to tears, turned his back on the scene. He could not believe his uncle just left him here. Again, he wondered why he was unable to make Bear Walker understand. The positive feelings he just experienced toward his uncle were gone in an instant.

I did not ask to be crippled, Mawatani thought. *I did not ask the Thunderbeings to kill my father.* The anger stayed with him, along with fear. He was left here, defenseless. Even if he was able to defend himself, he had no implement to use. He knew what Bear Walker would have to say about that: "You must be responsible for yourself. Why didn't you bring your hunting knife." He remembered having it in his hand to bring, then changing his mind. He wished now, it was by his side. He wished many things over the last year, but wishing was a waste of time, he decided. It never changes anything.

He loosened the strap from his bedroll and found the only dry, level place to lay it flat, was next to a tree; a tree split in two, with only half still remaining. He shivered as he realized this was the exact spot where his father was killed. This is what was left of the tree that changed his life.

The half tree still stood, now dead. Looking up at it, Mawatani felt akin to this pitiful remnant of a once proud and strong creature of Grandmother Earth. He too, was now only a half creature and felt part of him was dead. The other half of the tree that crippled him, still lay there, seemingly innocent of the havoc it caused.

This was a terrible place; a place of death and near death, yet, he sensed a sudden closeness to his father here. He felt a bond he had not felt with anyone since his father's death. It was as though he could almost touch his father's spirit.

Across the creek, Bear Walker already had a fire going, and was now walking into the trees with his bow.

Where is he going? Mawatani wondered. *I am now even more vulnerable. He acts as though I don't even exist.*

Mawatani sat on his bedroll, feeling loss, dread and loneliness, but savoring the feeling of connection he felt with his father. He stared at the purple and orange sunset, tracing the silver around the clouds with his eyes. *This was my atés favorite time of day.*

His heart was full as he reminisced about the times his father would stand in silence, watching the colors and shapes change as the sun set. Steals Many Horses told him the Great Spirit sent many messages in the sunset; you only had to learn to read them. But his father was not there to teach him now. He would probably never learn to read the language of the sunset.

The bond he felt was short lived. The sunset now became only a reminder of his loss. The anger and self-pity within him took too much room. There was little space left to allow good feelings to remain.

He lay, staring at the sky above, watching the shapes and colors disappear into the darkness. He wondered why he was made to live out this terrible life. *The Great Spirit has given death to the tree. It was not forced to live as half a tree. Am I not as important as this tree?*

The rolling in his stomach reminded him he was hungry. He did not feel like searching for roots.

The turnips they passed were too far away and the juneberry bushes were just sprouting, far from bearing fruit. He reached into his parfleche and pulled out a piece of pemmican; a *poor substitute for rabbit,* he thought.

As he lay there, the clean, earthy smell of the surroundings began to lose prominence, as the familiar, mouth-watering aroma of roasting rabbit spread across the creek. He knelt on his bedroll watching his Uncle turn the meat on the spit. The scene and inviting smell caused more memories to flood within him, not even giving him a chance to control the tears that welled from within.

As the silent tears flowed, the moonlight easily made its way through the sparse trees, causing his face to glisten like a rich brown rock, polished by the swift-flowing creek.

Though the aroma of the rabbit filled the air and made Mawatani's mouth water, the long trip and his emotions finally caught up with him. He could no longer fight the exhaustion. He was cold and his cheeks felt stiff from the salt of his tears, but he was too tired to care. Curling up in his bedroll, he tried to find a comfortable position. His leg ached as if it had been beaten. It was no longer accustomed to what it had been through today.

He listened to the night birds and could feel the power of the rushing waters a few feet from him. *Even the creek is powerful. Why can't I have some of that power?*

Across the creek, Bear Walker was cleaning up after his meal. By the time he finished, Mawatani rested in a deep sleep.

Chapter 5

No Time To Be Lame

The man and boy, separated more by perception than a creek, slept soundly on Grandmother Earth. They were lulled by the harmonious ensemble of nocturnal life and the flowing waters of the Cankpe Opi Wakpala.

A terrifying howl shattered the peaceful sounds of the night. Mawatani woke with a start. At first he could not identify the source of the sound. Then, from across the creek, he heard an outcry from his Uncle's camp. Pain surged through his leg as he forced himself to his feet. In the shadows from the moon-light and the flames and embers from Bear Walker's fire, he could see a large form crouching over the area where Bear Walker lay.

"Até! What is happening?"

Only the clamor of thrashing from across the creek was heard in reply: then, Bear Walker cried out in terror.

"Mawatani, it's a sakehanska; a grizzly bear!"

"I'm coming, Uncle." Without thinking further, Mawatani grabbed his bow and quiver and staggered into the creek and began to cross. He could see little but found the water shallow near the shore. Suddenly, the bottom disappeared, and he flailed his arms in an attempt to stay afloat. The icy water made his leg useless, but even so, he realized he was progressing.

In the tenuous moonlight, he saw the distance to the opposite shore grow shorter. Soon, solid ground lay beneath his feet. He had crossed the creek.

Dragging his leg, he rushed to his uncle, who was lying on his stomach, writhing in pain. The bear paused, turning to see what was interrupting her attack.

Bear Walker's robe was pulled off and his shirts lay in tattered shreds. Teeth and claw marks covered his back. When he realized that his nephew was there, he turned onto his back. Mawatani gasped at the sight. His Uncle's chest lay open. His flesh was ripped starting at the right side of his neck, across his chest to the bottom of the left side of his rib cage. Blood flowed freely from the horrific gash.

Mawatani hobbled into action, as the bear returned to her attack. Raising his bow and an arrow, his mind filled with all he had been taught about bears. *I must get to its throat. That is where they are the most vulnerable.*

Picking up a still flaming branch from the fire, Mawatani approached the crouching bear and thrust the burning branch onto the back of its neck, hoping the creature would turn and expose his throat. Barely feeling the burning flesh of his hand, he turned to move away. His leg gave out and he fell. Scrambling to his feet, he fixed an arrow to the bow.

At first, there was no response from the animal but, as the fur began to burn to the flesh, she reared up, attempting to reach the searing pain. Standing upright, she towered over the boy.

Mawatani was ready. He did not think of the hours of practice spent with his bow in previous years, but his body remembered well. The excitement and fear of the moment added strength as he held the nock of the arrow against the taut sinew string.

His body screamed in pain as the burned flesh of his hand pulled the string of the bow back, but he did not utter a sound. His muscles strained and ached from lack of use as he aimed the arrow at the bear's exposed throat. Mawatani continued to pull until he was sure the tension was as firm as he could make it. Penetrating the bear's tough hide was imperative. Their lives depended on how this arrow left the bow.

The bear, angry and in pain, turned toward him and began to lunge.

Mawatani's aim was true. The arrow pierced the bear's throat. There was a raspy gasp as blood spurted through the air. With her paws clawing at the arrow, the animal attempted to pull it out, but it was imbedded through the back of her neck. Falling to the ground, her body burning and blood pouring out of her throat, she writhed in pain and fear.

Mawatani went to Bear Walker, pulling him away from the burning animal. He did not know what to do next. The bear was fatally wounded, he was sure of that, but she would not die. As long as she was alive, she was still dangerous.

Scanning the campsite, Mawatani's eyes stopped at the sight of Bear Walker's knife. Never, had he felt such fear. Taking the knife in his blistered hand, he tried to find a way to the bear's throat as she rolled on the ground in tormented spasms. She had been successful in putting out some of the flames, but too much of her body was aflame to get it all.

Mawatani wanted to kill her, not only for their safety, but because no creature of the earth should have to endure such pain.

Finding an opening, he found strength that he was sure he did not have. "Be with me, Tunkasila. Hokahe!" Mawatani charged the tormented bear, lunging the knife into her already ravaged throat, completely severing the windpipe. The animal convulsed and fell to the ground, finally free from pain. Mawatani removed the knife, wiped it off on the grass and placed it in his belt.

The smell of burning fur and flesh filled the air. The struggle had silenced the creatures of the night. The only sounds that broke the stillness were the soft moaning of Bear Walker, and the rushing waters of the Cankpe Opi Wakpala. His life drained away in red pools.

Mawatani slipped out of his leggings and carefully wrapped them around his uncle's chest, attempting to close the wound and slow the flow of blood. That was not enough. He scooped up mud from the edge of the creek and applied it over the gaping wound, which helped to further slow the bleeding. Cutting vines that grew up and around the trees nearest the water, he carefully tied them around other deep wounds that bled.

Bear Walker painfully smiled at him. His words came haltingly.

"Perhaps this was not the safest spot," he whispered. His smile increased as he said, "Mawatani, I am so proud of you. You are indeed a brave. The Great Spirit did help me to find a way to show you who you could be."

Mawatani felt the fear and understood the real danger he had encountered, but he did not have time to allow himself to think about it. He only was aware that he must get help.

"Pilamaya, Uncle. Thank you. I must get you to a safe place and go for help. You need powerful medicine now."

He recalled a small cave he and his father discovered on one of their trips here. It was not much more than a hollow in a little rise downstream;

too small for bears to use, but big enough to place his uncle. But, how would he get him there?

Then he remembered Bear Walker pointing out an old abandoned canoe as they passed along the side of the creek where the water turned. It was not far from where they entered the trees. The boat was old and probably leaked, but it might float well enough to get Bear Walker to the shelter.

"I will leave for a while, Uncle. I must get you to a safer place before I go for help." His mind flashed back to how his father's body had disappeared. He did not want that to happen again.

Covering Bear Walker with his tattered robe, he turned to leave. He wondered if he should take time to douse the flames of the still burning animal. *No,* he decided. *The flames will keep my uncle warm and keep other four-leggeds away.*

The soft breeze in the cold night air penetrated the wet shirts Mawatani wore. The thought of keeping Bear Walker warm made him realize how cold he was. He had no robe; it was still on the other side of the creek. His leggings were being used to hold his Uncle's body together.

Carefully, he pulled down Bear Walker's robe, took the remnants of one of the shirts and replaced the robe. He began to tie the material around his bad leg but thought better of it. *I have to cross the creek to get to the canoe. I'll cross now and get my robe.* He headed back to his camp, holding the tattered shirt high enough to keep it dry.

When he first crossed, he did not notice the thin layer of ice that sporadically lined the edges of the creek. For some reason, it made it seem even colder now.

Hampered by fatigue, his throbbing leg, and a badly burned hand, it was difficult to keep the remnant of the shirt dry, as the water splashed around him; but it was necessary. He had to have something to warm his leg. He would never get his uncle to safety and find help if he was not able to bring his leg to life again, and soon.

Painfully, he struggled onto the shore, gasping for breath. His lungs felt as though they would burst. He went toward his bedroll, exhausted, and knelt for a time, gulping large quantities of air. For a moment, all thought left him except for the pain he was experiencing. His burning hand felt as though it was still in the fire. His leg throbbed, and his whole body ached. After a moment he realized, *I cannot give in to this pain. I must get help for Bear Walker.*

Using dirt in his unburned hand, Mawatani rubbed his leg to dry it, then wrapped it with the torn shirt, protecting it from the frigid air. He threw his robe around his shoulders and headed off toward the abandoned canoe, calling to his uncle that he would return soon.

He had gone only a few steps when he stopped. *I must ask for help from those who are our guides; the Wakanpi, the Spirits,* he thought. For a silent moment, he stood with arms raised towards the skies, but prayer would not come. *I no longer know how to pray,* he thought. *If the spirits are real, they will know what is in my heart.* Quickly, he resumed his way to the canoe.

As he hurried along the creek with his leg dragging, he made a mental list of all he must do. First, he must get to the canoe. He prayed that it would be useable. Then, somehow, he must get Bear Walker into the canoe. Hopefully, he could remember exactly where the hollow was. He would have to find material to block the entrance to the hollow to keep out other four-leggeds. After all that was accomplished, he would have to get word to Night Eagle's village. If it was daylight by then, he could use smoke signals; if not, he would have to get to the village.

He was exhausted. *I have no time to be tired. I will have to be tired later.*

PART II
THE AWAKENING

Chapter 6

. . . .

The Vigil

The glow of anpo wicahpi, the morning star, was fading with the rising of the sun, bringing hazy light to the people of Night Eagle's village. People in the camp were doing their chores in their winter robes. Warmth had not come with the morning light today.

Along with the usual sounds of the start of day, the cadence of soft drums, rattles, and the droning of prayerful chants mingled with the crisp air. These sounds rose to join the smoke ascending from the lodges, filling the universe with its pulse and songs of prayer.

The rhythm and chants came from the medicine lodge of Hears The Voice, a bear dreamer, who healed with his spiritual medicine. He had been sending his voice to Wakan Tanka, the Great Spirit, throughout the night for the healing of Bear Walker.

Also keeping vigil was Walks In Silence, who knew all there was to know about Lakdwapayapi, the medicines that come from Grandmother Earth. He had cleansed each wound with hente pejuta, a disinfectant made from cedar, then carefully applied taopi pejuta, a healing salve of turtle heart and tobacco. For the swelling, he used a salve of poip'iye pejuta, made from white plantain, a common shrub. To help with pain, he applied wahpataya pejuta, made from snakeroot.

Outside of prayers to the Great Spirit and to mitakuye oyasin, this was the strongest medicine they had.

A wanbli wapiya, a man whose healing power came from the eagle, had also been in the lodge throughout the night. These holy men combined their powers to send a strong message to Tunkasila, the being beyond knowing, and to Wakan Tanka, whose mystery was beyond all understanding.

The still body of Bear Walker lay between them, clinging to life. The chants of these holy men explained to Wakan Tanka that it was very important this man, lying before them, be healed. The boy who saved his life had already lost his father. Mawatani needed his uncle to remain here to guide him.

The men thanked the Great Mystery for the story of this brave koskolaka. It would be a good story for the children to hear, and for their children's children. They hoped the young men of their village would learn from this deed.

Nearby, an inipi lodge was being prepared so others could join them with the sacred pipe. They would purify themselves through the sacred rite of the inipi, the ceremony of the sweat lodge. There, they would send their voices to the Great Spirit.

Night Eagle sat in his lodge within a circle of elders. "What message are the spirits giving Mawatani and Bear Walker? Are the people no longer welcome in the trees? It is strange that tragedy would strike twice at the same site."

"Perhaps the bad medicine of the evil spirits has spread its robe there," an elder suggested.

"If that is true, can the area be reclaimed through sacrifice and ceremony?" asked Night Eagle. "I will have to discuss these thoughts with Talks With Owls. I understand he is very knowledgeable about such things."

Outside, children, bundled in buffalo robes, gathered around a nearby tipi, talking quietly about the boy inside; the boy who killed a bear.

Inside the tipi, Mawatani slept. He arrived at the village early yesterday morning. He insisted upon returning to Bear Walker with the rescue party.

Soon after the men placed his uncle's battered body on a travois for his return to Night Eagle's village, Mawatani fell asleep. The boy was exhausted. His throbbing leg refused to carry him any longer. Though his body ached, and his blistered hand felt as though it was still in the fire, the fatigue he experienced overtook the pain and he slept well.

A woman, who was with him through the night, stirred a pot of acorn mush, keeping it warm for when he woke. Several times, over the last few minutes, she noticed the boy moving. He would wake soon.

As sleep left him, Mawatani first felt the terrible ache that was his leg. When he began to move, his body was stiff and sore. As he reached to rub his leg, he realized his hand was bound. It was then he became aware of the unfamiliar setting. The smells were unlike those he usually woke to, though the aroma of the acorn mush was particularly inviting.

Mawatani's eyes opened slightly. The parfleche, hanging next to him was unfamiliar. Carefully guarding his leg, he slowly and painfully turned on his back. His eyes met those of a woman he knew. This was Singing Lark, the wife of Eagle Eyes. She was the woman who cared for him last year; who had been so gentle and kind.

He began to rise, but his body balked from exhaustion and -pain.

As the woman gently placed her hand on his shoulder, Mawatani remembered Bear Walker.

"Até!" Where is my Uncle?" he asked.

"Your Uncle lives", Singing Lark answered. "He still sleeps."

"I must see him. Where is he?" Slowly, Mawatani stood. His hands went to his weak and painful leg, which he rubbed in an attempt to find relief.

"Bear Walker is in the medicine lodge with my husband and two other medicine men. They must not be disturbed. The inipi lodge is being prepared for others who want to send their voices to the Great Spirit for your uncle."

"I will join them in the inipi," Mawatani insisted.

"You are too tired and weak for that now. Perhaps you can stay with your uncle while they share the pipe. For now, you will eat."

Mawatani was hungry. He had eaten nothing since those few bites of pemmican on the first night. A whole day and night had passed since then.

As he began to eat, two young heads poked into the opening of the lodge.

Singing Lark shooed them with her hands.

"We want to see Mawatani," one said.

"We want to hear his story and talk to him," said another. The other children outside began to shout in excitement.

"Perhaps later, he will talk to you," Singing Lark answered. "Now he is eating."

The youngsters backed away and returned to their friends.

"Why do they want to talk to me?" Mawatani asked.

"You are a hero, Mawatani", Singing Lark replied. "You saved your uncle's life. You killed the bear that was attacking him. Few braves can make that claim."

"That does not make me a hero, Mawatani said. I did only what had to be done; only what they would have done."

Singing Lark closed her eyes and a slight smile formed. When her eyes opened, her face reflected the gentleness and wisdom that were known and loved by the villagers.

"Mawatani, you are now a koskolaka; a young man barely beyond a small child. Your thoughts were quick and mature. You quickly made decisions and acted upon them, not hindered by fear. You are, indeed, a hero. The story of what you have done will be told many times. You are a good hero for our hoksilas. Young boys need good heroes."

Mawatani was startled by her comments. What he did seemed so natural and, though he felt pride in killing the bear, he did not feel heroic. The only thing he felt was the wonderful feeling of knowing he might be able to contribute to his village after all. He had not felt this since that horrible day last year. It was a good feeling.

"My mother and the rest of our village will be wondering where we are," Mawatani said. "We should be home soon."

"A wahosiyapi has gone to your village to let them know you are with us," Singing Lark told him.

It is good they sent a messenger to my village, Mawatani thought. *My mother and Bear Walker's family would be concerned when we failed to return on time.*

After he ate, Singing Lark and Mawatani went to the medicine lodge to see Bear Walker. The boy walked gingerly, attempting to hide his pain.

The children who were keeping vigil outside, began to follow.

"Mawatani," a young boy called, "will you tell us your story now?"

Mawatani turned to him. "I'm going to see my uncle now and be with him during the inipi. We will

49

have time after that if you really want to hear the story."

"We do, we do," the children shouted.

"Then I will come to you after the inipi."

"When?" a hoksila asked.

"Toksa," Mawatani answered, letting them know it would be a little while.

The experience of feeling a part of life again was wonderful.

His leg did not feel so good now, however. His limp was worse than usual; there was no way to hide it.

Inside the lodge, the three holy men brought their healing ceremony to a close. They greeted Mawatani with great respect and told him that Bear Walker was fortunate to have such a brave nephew. As they spoke, a young brave came to tell them that the initi, the sweat lodge, was ready.

In respect, each man placed his hand on Mawatani's shoulders as they left the lodge.

Mawatani's heart felt as though it would burst from pride, another feeling absent for a long time; a feeling he never expected to experience again.

Looking at his Uncle, he cringed. Bear Walker looked terrible. His skin was grayish; corpselike. Except for the slight movement of his chest, from his shallow breathing, Mawatani would have thought he was dead. As he stared into his uncle's face, he thought of all the times Bear Walker had lost patience with him during the last months. He also thought of his rude and cowardly responses to him.

He remembered his own times of anger, disappointment, and even disbelief that his father's brother would be so lacking in understanding of his condition.

Now I understand why my Uncle was right to be disappointed in me. I am able to do things I have not even dreamed of doing since the tree fell on me. I am not crippled. I have been acting like a wacinko. I have been so involved in feeling sorry for myself because of what I could no longer do, I forgot to find out what I could do.

Chapter 7

· · · · · · · · · · · · · · · · · · · ·

The Healing Begins

Five days passed since Mawatani and Bear Walker were brought to Night Eagle's village. The medicine Bear Walker received was good. By the third day, he regained consciousness and his many wounds were beginning to heal. Much additional time would be needed to truly mend his body, but the process had begun. Plans were being made for their return home.

Hears The Voice and Bear Walker spoke about the year since the death of Steals Many Horses, and how the boy withdrew from life. Bear Walker told him of his plan to return with the boy to the area of the death and injury. He spoke of his prayer to the Great Spirit, asking for aid in finding a way to help the boy rediscover life and his part in it.

Hears The Voice marveled at how the spirits had answered Bear Walker's prayer. He agreed that, even if Bear Walker had not lived, the loss of his life would have been a welcome exchange for the awakening of Mawatani.

Night Eagle was particularly excited by the story. He no longer worried about evil spirits taking over the area of the rabbits. From this story, he decided that it was now a holy place.

Hears The Voice watched Mawatani with great interest over the last few days. Several times he saw the boy with the young children of the village. He appeared to be shy, but comfortable with them and was kind and gentle as they flocked around him.

Mawatani was reveling in being part of life again. He felt a part of this community and was thankful for that feeling. He was not comfortable, however, with the heroic image the villagers had placed on him. Some people, young and old, were calling him Bear Killer.

Hoksilas and koskolakas always cherished the opportunity to speak of their heroic deeds. That was part of being a boy; how you gained respect. Being humble was usually considered cowardly. *What I did may be considered heroic by some*, Mawatani thought, *but it was not*.

He never understood the concept of heroism. Being brave, he understood. To him, if something needed to be done, you did it. It didn't matter if was making an arrowhead or killing a bear. Life was full of everyday tasks and danger. One was no more heroic than the other. He knew of no others who thought this way.

Many of the women were calling him Hoksila Wakan, Holy Boy, because he was so soft-spoken and did not want to accept his heroism.

I am certainly not holy. I have forfeited any rights to a new name by my behavior and actions during this last year. A new name must be earned by changing the way I live. It is time for igluhomni. I must turn myself around. This was a word he heard used many times during his life. He never understood what it meant, until now.

One good or even brave deed cannot make up for this year of uncountable wrong deeds. It cannot possibly erase the hurt I caused my family and my tiyospaye. Yes, I must turn myself around.

As eager as he was to see his mother and siblings, a feeling of anxiety about his return weighed heavily on him. How could he face them? How could he possibly explain his behavior?

I did not support my mother at all when my até was killed; when she needed me the most. Even when my grandmother died, I thought only of my loss, not hers. It must have been so hard for her. How can I ever make up for the way I have treated my family; not just my mother and brothers and sister, but the whole tiyospaye? I have been hateful, cruel and cowardly. Why didn't I see it sooner? Why didn't I listen to what Bear Walker told me over and over for the last year? My behavior almost cost Bear Walker his life. Now I understand. Mawatani had much to think and to pray about.

Hears The Voice and the other men decided that Bear Walker was now well enough to travel. Several members of the village arranged to accompany the two to their village the next day.

To celebrate Bear Walker's healing and honor his nephew, tonight there would be a gathering. There was much for which to be thankful. There was no better way to celebrate than with dancing, singing, and the sending of voices to Tunkasila, the Creator Grandfather.

Chapter 8

The Return

The gathering lasted far into the night. Mawatani felt as though he just crawled into bed when Singing Lark woke him. Night Eagle wanted them to get an early start. Their travel would proceed slowly, because Bear Walker's wounds were still open, and they did not want them to begin bleeding again. He would be strapped to a travois. The faster they moved, the more it would bounce. Walks In Silence placed a small bush under each pole to limit the bouncing.

Mawatani had mixed feelings about returning home. One moment, he was excited, looking forward to seeing his family and friends. He also wondered if he still had any friends. *Will my family really be glad to see me? It has probably been quite peaceful there without me.*

Stepping outside the lodge, Mawatani was surprised to see how many were going with them. He thought it would probably be just Hears The Voice and one or two others, but there were several men and women joining them. They were packing a travois with gifts for the old and poor in Mawatani's village.

Mawatani's attention was so fixed on the preparations to leave, he didn't even notice the boy who rode up behind him, holding the reins to another horse.

"Bear Killer," the boy cried out. "What is mine is now yours. Sunkawakan cic'u kte. I give you this horse."

Mawatani turned, and his eyes beheld a marvelous sight. The boy held the reins to a second horse; a mustang as beautiful as he had ever seen. Against a pure white coat, rich brown markings ran down his flanks and along his back. His head, marked with an elongated diamond, was held high as he pranced in a side-wise gait alongside the young boy's horse.

"I captured and broke him myself," the boy announced. "Here," he said, handing the reins to Mawatani, "he is now yours."

Astounded, Mawatani stood open-mouthed, gazing at this beautiful creature and at the boy who held the reins. He had seen him several times during his stay, but they never spoke. This was the boy who seemed to always stay apart from the group. Mawatani knew his name only because he heard a man call him.

"I have never seen a more beautiful horse, Zicahota."

"He is beautiful," Zicahota replied. "I have taken good care of him."

"That is obvious. It is a wonderful gift and I accept it with great humility."

Zicahota slid off his horse and placed his hand on Mawatani's shoulders. "It is my honor to give him to you."

Those waiting to join in the return of Bear Walker and Mawatani, all marveled at what just took place. Zicahota was not known for his generosity. It took him months to capture and train this horse and he took great pride in him.

"I have learned much from what you have said and done,

Mawatani," Zicahota said. "My prayer is that we will become friends."

"I will cherish that friendship, Zicahota," Mawatani replied. "Will you come with us on our return home?"

"Yes," Zicahota answered quickly, his eyes shining with excitement. "I will get my bundle and be right back." He jumped on his horse and quickly rode to his lodge.

The villagers shook their heads in wonder. Zicahota's parents were in awe. They could hardly believe what they just saw. Even his father was seldom able to carry on a conversation with his son. The boy usually stayed to himself, honing his riding skills, or target shooting. His skill with the bow surpassed many men of the village. He seldom spoke unless first spoken to.

The only real relationship Zicahota had formed was with his sister, Kimimila, a girl of ten years. As their custom demanded, he had not spoken to her since he was seven. He showed his love by being especially protective of her. Many young boys had learned not to tease her when he was around.

Zicahota's father was stunned, but incredibly pleased. He decided this moment was holy. He too, would travel with the group. When he returned, he would ask others to join him to share the pipe and thank the spirits who moved his son to do such a generous thing.

Mawatani was pleased to have someone his own age on the return home. The time would pass more quickly.

Men came from the lodge of Hears The Voice carrying Bear Walker. They carefully laid him on the travois, securing the blanket to the frame.

As they were ready to pull out, Night Eagle came out to say goodbye and wish the travelers well.

He told them he sent a wahsosiyapi, a messenger ahead to let Bear Walker's camp know that he and Mawatani would be home this day. He also told them one of their braves went back to the site of the attack and found a yearling bear cub wandering nearby. Apparently, this was the cub of the bear that attacked Bear Walker. Undoubtedly, the bear was just protecting her cub.

"What will happen to the cub now?" Mawatani asked.

"It learned much from its mother last year. It will probably do well," Night Eagle answered.

Hears The Voice gave the signal to move out.

Zicahota had not yet returned. Mawatani signaled he would wait for his new friend and catch up with them.

The wait was short. Zicahota came barreling out of his tipi and jumped on his horse before the party even passed the circle of lodges.

The pace was slow. Several times Hears The Voice stopped to cut small bushes to replace those that had worn down under the poles of the travois. They served their purpose well in softening the ride.

Mawatani and Zicahota talked some, but mostly enjoyed each other's company. When they talked, it was mainly about the horse that was now Mawatani's.

"I decided this horse would someday be mine the first time I saw him," Zicahota said. "He was almost too clever for me. Many times I thought I had him within my grasp, but he would get away each time. He would look back at me as though I was a fool to think I could catch him. He led his pack well and protected his herd. He is a true sunkawakan, Mawatani; a horse more holy than any I have ever seen."

"I will call him Napasni," Mawatani announced, "for he is strong and brave."

"It is a good name, Bear Killer," his friend agreed.

Several times during the trip, the boys would leave the party and chase after jack rabbits or lizards or whatever ran or crawled on Grandmother Earth. The companionship was good.

Mawatani's body still ached and his burned hand still throbbed. At the moment, all this seemed unimportant. He forgot how good it was to have friends. He would not forget again.

Chapter 9

. . . .

The Welcome

Just before dusk, a young boy, playing by the creek near Mawatani's village, saw the group from Night Eagle's village as they were entering the camp. "Wan He! Look over there! Kupelo! Here they come!"

Soon all the children saw them. "Agli! Agli! Agli wanyanka" they began to yell, "Mawatani and Bear Walker! Agli! They have returned!"

Villagers came to welcome the visitors and rejoice in the return of their own. Holy Moon Woman saw her son. The look of pride her face revealed filled Mawatani with feelings that almost overwhelmed him. There were feelings of incredible love and joy mixed with painful shame.

As his family stood before him, he wanted to throw his arms around his mother and each of his siblings, but he knew he was too old for that; at least in public. He was not sure he could contain himself once they were alone in their lodge.

As they rode further into the camp, the smaller children crowded around Mawatani, begging him to tell his story.

Several young boys, including his two closest friends, rode up to him, their faces unsmiling, somber and distant. Mawatani halted Napasni and looked at the cold eyes of his peers. He could see his thoughts of earlier in the day had been correct. He no longer had friends here. Just as that was beginning to sink in, his cousin, Catches Tail, snorted and began to laugh. They had tricked him. This caused the other boys to lose control, and soon their laughter was taken up by the villagers.

"Hau, Kola!" Six Toes called in friendship.

Catches Tail brought his horse next to Mawatani. He leaned over and placed his hand on his cousin's shoulder. "It is good you have returned to us, Mawatani. You have been away for many moons. We missed you."

Mawatani did not understand at first. He was gone only seven sleeps. Then he realized his friend was speaking of the past year. That, he could understand. The boy he was during that time was also a stranger to himself.

"Hyaa-a-a," Mawatani sang in thanks. "Pilamaya. Thank you. We must speak of this later," though he had no idea what he would say.

Mawatani forgot how tired he was from last night's gathering. The excitement of the moment caused his body to forget its exhaustion as he introduced his friends to Zicahota.

"Do you see this beautiful horse? Zicahota has given him to me. Can you believe it?"

His friends were amazed by this remarkable gift from someone he barely knew.

"You are fortunate to have received such a gift," Six Toes said. "I have never seen a horse with more beauty."

"Hey, Wacinko."

The voice could not be mistaken. Etonka, listening nearby, rode up to Mawatani. He looked at Napasni, then back to Mawatani.

"What's the matter poor little boy?" Etonka asked. "Are you too frightened or lazy to catch your own horse? You must be to accept one from someone you don't even know."

"And how many bears have you killed?" asked Zicahota. "I am interested in why you believe Mawatani is frightened or lazy. He has just saved his uncle's life by killing a bear with his hands. To me, that does not sound like someone frightened or lazy."

"I have killed no bears," Etonka answered, "and I doubt if Mawatani has either. There must have been others there. He could not have done this himself."

"I see," said Zicahota. "Then he is making up this story, as is Bear Walker." Looking defiantly at Etonka, Zicahota said, "You are foolish to think this. Their wounds are real. I gave Mawatani this horse because I respected what he did. He is one of the bravest persons I have ever known. In my village he is treated with honor."

"In this village also," yelled Catches Tail. The young people began to whoop and trill and the adults joined in. Etonka's face flushed and he turned his horse and galloped away from the crowd.

The wonderful feeling of belonging flowed through Mawatani's body; energizing him, as he watched all his people. Many gathered around Bear Walker and the visitors.

Glancing at the crowd, Mawatani saw Holy Moon Woman, who still stood nearby. *Ina...my mother*, he thought. His love for her swelled within him until he thought he would burst. Her smile was full of love, pride and thankfulness. He had not seen that look for a long time and could think of nothing more beautiful at the moment; not even Napasni. He did not even try to control the smile that appeared.

Still sitting on Napasni, Mawatani raised his eyes to the skies.

"Hyaa-a-a! Hyaa-a-a!" he cried to Tunkasila. "Pilamaya, Great Spirit. Thank you for helping me find my life again. Help me to help my people."

The people all turned toward him, most of them not hearing what he said. Those who heard rejoiced and sent their voices to Wakan Tanka for this wonderful day.

Preparation for the welcome home began as soon as the tiyospaye learned Mawatani and Bear Walker were on their way. Though fresh buffalo meat was unavailable at this time because of the flood, the women always found a way of preparing feasts when the occasion called for it.

Fortunately, only the day before, three young braves came across a group of elk that stopped downstream from the camp. In a short time, two were killed, butchered and returned to the village.

There was still a supply of dried berries, turnips, onions and roots to use for seasoning. Cooked with the fat from the elk, there would be plenty of tasty food for the celebration this evening.

Later, the men from Night Eagle's village were asked to tell all they knew about the story of Mawatani and Bear Walker. When they finished, men raised Bear Walker's back slightly so he could speak. Breathing and talking were difficult, but with pride, he told what he remembered. At the end of each story, the women would warble and trill, and the men shouted and chanted their approval.

When Bear Walker finished, Mawatani was asked to tell his story. He was hesitant to stand before the people of his village, feeling much shame.

Quickly, he told his story, leaving out much of what he had done. He told the tiyospaye how thankful they should be for the healing powers of Hears The Voice and Walks In Silence. "Their medicine was very powerful," he told them. "I was sure I would lose Bear Walker, as I lost my father."

He used this opportunity to speak about something much more important to him. He spoke to his people of the shame he felt for his behavior during the last year.

"I will have one aim in my life for the moons to come: igluhomni," Mawatani announced. "I will turn myself around. Wanmayanka yo! Look at me! Wacintankpo. Be patient with me. I will make it up to you. Wakuyelo.I have returned to you, not just from a trip to the trees, but from the grasp of the bad spirits. I ask Talk With Owls to help me find myself again, and rid myself of these evil spirits. I ask all of you to send your voices to Tunkasila to help me in this. Wahowaye; I promise this is what I will do."

Talks With Owls was pleased and nodded his approval.

Hears The Voice asked to speak last. He spoke of his time with Bear Walker and his talks with Mawatani.

"This hoksila...no...this koskolaka has many gifts from the spirits. This you should know. Someday, all our oyate, the people of our nation, will know of Mawatani and will look to him for wisdom and counsel."

When the talking was finished, the dancing began and continued into the night. Even Mawatani attempted to join in, but it was not long before his leg would no longer cooperate with his body. Still exhausted from the night before, he decided to go to his lodge and sleep. He invited Zicahota to sleep in his lodge when he was ready. Mawatani was in a deep sleep when his friend returned.

Again, morning came quickly. After much friendly leave-taking, Hears The Voice and the other visitors began their return home, laden with gifts. They were no more than a speck on the horizon when Zicahota finally said his last goodbye to Mawatani. Moments before, Mawatani ran to his lodge and took his father's bow and quiver from its place on the wall. *Zicahota has given me his most precious possession. I will give him mine.*

"This has been a good time, Bear Killer," Zicahota said.

"It has been a great time," Mawatani replied. "I have made a good new friend. I have something for you." He handed his treasure to his friend.

"Your father's bow? I thank you for this special gift." Zicahota knew how much this bow meant to Mawatani; he had shown it to him in his lodge this morning. "I will use it well, Mawatani."

Mawatani nodded. "I hope it will help you kill many buffalo. Before you go, I have a favor to ask."

"Ask," his friend replied.

"I ask that you call me Mawatani, not Bear Killer."

"Why? Did you not kill a bear?" asked Zicahota.

"Yes, I killed a bear, but I don't feel comfortable with that name. It is not right for me."

"Ahh...but it is right to me," replied Zicahota, "Until you earn a more Fitting name, I will call you Bear Killer. It is a good name." With that, he jumped on his horse and galloped off to meet the others.

As his friend disappeared on the horizon, Mawatani became aware of all the activity taking place around him. Life was going on; a life he had forgotten how to live. There were women washing, mending, preparing food and visiting; men meeting, working, discussing, deciding and praying.

Without warning, a sudden feeling of loneliness and fear swept over him. The festivities were over, the visitors gone. Now he had to be a part of everyday life again. He had to figure out how he was going to live up to the promise he made the night before. Was he really up to it?

He promised to turn his life around. Igluhomni: a word that usually meant facing a different direction. It also had another meaning: changing your attitude. The meaning never meant much to him; it was just a word. Nw it was an action he must take. He had no idea how to begin.

PART III

IGLUHOMNI-THE SPIRIT IS
ONLY SOMETIMES WILLING

Chapter 10

• •

Rejoining

The spring rains and floods sent the buffalo far from their usual grazing grounds and rutting areas. The hunt would have to go well into the territory of their enemy, the Arikara, to locate any now. That was too far for many of the older members of the tiyospaye to travel. Besides, hunting on the Arikara lands would bring danger to young and old. They would not go hungry. The men found deer, elk, and moose. Downstream, flocks of ducks and geese stopped to rest on their way to their summer homes. Fish were plentiful in the creek. The real need now, was for Buffalo skins.

There was one emergency now, however. A fire the day before had taken everything but the lives of one family. It not only destroyed their tipi, but all of their belongings.

Holy Moon Woman and Tahcawe worked with some of the other women and girls. They were piecing together skins that had been donated to form a makeshift temporary tipi until the summer hunt. Others were preparing deer and elk skin to make clothing.

Some of the men and boys sifted through the ashes for arrowheads and other reusable items. Others prepared wood for a bow or rounded shafts for arrows to replace those destroyed. Bear Walker was healing well and joined in the work, doing what he could.

Mawatani sat with some of his friends, smoothing an arrow shaft. Though a few stubborn blisters persisted, the worst burns were healing well. He was doing his best to get back into the rhythm of life and wasn't about to let a couple of blisters stop him from helping.

Mawatani's head was full of things that needed reflection. At times, he still felt a hunger to be alone. It was hard to grab a few minutes by himself to be attentive to his thoughts. In the days since the visitors brought them home, he took every moment he could find to try to sort things out.

Over the past year he became accustomed to spending time alone whenever he felt like it. Since his return, he felt guilty when he wanted to be alone. He was afraid that if he did go off by himself, the people would think he was reverting to his old behavior; but this was different. He did not want to be alone to escape from the others. He felt an urgent need to be alone to study the never-ending stream of thoughts that ran through his head.

Some things were clear now. Bear Walker had certainly been right about a lot of things; the fact that he was not really crippled and that he assumed there were things he could not do because he had been afraid to try them.

There were some things he knew he would never again be able to do well. He would no longer win the "hoop and pole" game or the "swing kicking" game; but he could participate. These games would help condition his body. With practice, he could still be competitive with the bow and arrow; of course, that would be after he made a new one. He was angry with himself for destroying his old bow and was using one of Bear Walker's old bows for now.

There was one thing in particular he wanted to think about. *What about the dreams I have been having the last few nights? They are no more than little snatches. They all take place in a huge, dark canyon. Sometimes there is lightning, but never the thunder to follow. There is nothing but darkness, then a few flashes of silent lightning.*

Often, just before I wake, an image appears. I think it is some form of animal, but I can never bring it into focus. In one of these dreams, during the silent thunder, a spirit appeared; no, not really appeared... I just felt its presence. No, that's not quite it either. It is as though this presence was flying in the silent lightning; like a bird, but it wasn't a bird... at least I don't think it was.

Maybe my dreams are a look into the future, not just a reminder of what has been. Perhaps these really are visions meant to guide me on my journey to adulthood, but how am I to find out? My dreams are nothing but little flashes; pieces of something that I am never able to grasp.

As these thoughts continued, he realized that someone was calling him.

"Mawatani! Where are your ears?" his cousin asked.

"I'm sorry," Mawatani replied. "I was just thinking of something. I didn't hear you."

A mischievous grin fell across the face of Catches Tail. "Ohhh," he said, looking at the other boys, "I bet I know what he was thinking about."

Then, looking at Mawatani, he said, "Zicahota told us he has a sister who thinks you are a great hero. In fact, she told him you were the finest looking Koskalaka within the Paha Sapa. Is that right, Mawatani? Are you the finest looking young man in the Sacred Black Hills?"

Six Toes entered in, "I bet his sister is beautiful and sweet like canhanpi. Isn't that right, Mawatani?"

"Oh yes. Is she sweet, like sugar, Mawatani?" asked another of his cousins.

Their teasing took Mawatani by surprise. He could feel a blush sweep over his face. "You tell a silly joke. No, that is not what I was thinking. I didn't even meet his sister. He did not tell you that."

"Oh yes he did," Six Toes taunted. The boys laughed at Mawatani's embarrassment.

"Well, I was thinking of something else, not a girl," Mawatani said. "Besides, she's only ten summers old."

"If you say so." Catches Tail's sly grin almost made Mawatani angry.

Etonka had been listening to all this. "What female would want a whiner, a cripple who sews parfleches and sits by the water feeling sorry for himself?"

Catches Tail rose in anger. "Etonka, we have heard enough from you. Have you ever walked in Mawatani's shoes? Have you ever felt the torment he has felt? Has your até been killed by the WAKINYAN? Has your leg been made almost useless by the hand of the WAKINYAN? Go somewhere else with your bad medicine, Etonka. We have heard all we will hear of your jealousy."

Etonka began to object, but the boys made it clear that they would have none of it. He turned and walked away, sulking.

Mawatani started to go after him to find out why he hated him so much, but Six Toes stopped him and shook his head. "Don't worry about him, Mawatani. He is acting like a small child. He is not worth your worry."

"When we're through here we're going to play the "ring and pin" game," Catches Tail said. "Do you want to play?"

Mawatani was hoping to find some time alone when he was through but felt he should join in the activities of his friends. He would really like to figure out the behavior of Etonka. He also wondered if he would even be able to throw a spear up to the ring. *Well, I won't know unless I try,* he decided.

"Sure, I'll play," he answered. He knew he was going to have to get used to losing most games for a while. Besides the actual injury to his leg, his body lost much of its quickness and agility during the last year. Some of it, he would probably never regain. But the more he did now, the better it would be.

The boys played until dinner time. Mawatani walked toward his lodge pleased that he did better than he expected. He didn't win by a long way, but he didn't come in last either. At the beginning, he couldn't hit the ring no matter how hard he tried. After they had played for a while, he was doing pretty well. It felt good. He would get better at it. He knew he would.

During the evening meal, Mawatani's mind began to fill with all the thoughts he had been trying to find time to think about. They raced through his head, not giving him a chance to capture them. He clutched at his head trying to grasp even one thought and bring it to rest. A heavy drowsiness overcame him like a blanket being tossed over his head. He crawled to his mat. By the time he lay on it, he was asleep. He heard his mother asking him what was wrong, but he was not able to respond. Then there was blackness and deep sleep.

Though Holy Moon Woman was frightened, she decided the excitement of the last few weeks finally caught up with him. He just needed sleep. He would be fine in the morning.

73

Chapter 11

The Long Silence

With morning, came the usual sounds of the start of day. There was the blend of songs from the various winged people above that accompanied the bustling activity of the encampment. From all appearances, the day was like any other, until the panicked voice of Holy Moon Woman was heard.

"Capa Winhaha, run and get Bear Walker! There is something wrong with Mawatani!"

Capa Winhaha dashed out of the tipi and ran toward Bear Walker's lodge. "Até! Uncle!" the boy called, as he approached the tipi. "Come help. Mawatani won't wake up."

Bear Walker quickly emerged from the tipi and ran ahead of the boy. He entered his nephew's tipi, went to the sleeping boy and shook him.

"How long has he been like this?" Bear Walker asked.

Holy Moon Woman explained how he became very sleepy early last evening and had been sleeping ever since.

"We will get Cankuwasté. He will know what to do. Capa Winhaha, go to his lodge and tell him he is needed."

Cankuwasté was a respected pejuta wicasa, a medicine man. He had brought cures to many of their people. He went immediately to Mawatani and knelt next to him. He touched the boy's head and body with his hands. He put his ear to the boy's chest, hearing and feeling the rhythms of the complex network the Great Spirit had woven to create His people.

Cankuwasté said, "His breath comes slowly, but it is even. His heart beats well and his body is not hot. Take him to the medicine lodge. There, I will do a healing ceremony and we will share the pipe."

Looking toward Holy Moon Woman, Cankuwasté said, "I will send my voice to the spirits and perform all the healing rites. Stay strong, Holy Moon Woman. He will return."

In Cankuwasté's lodge, the pipe was shared. The sound of chants and rattles of the rite were heard, but Mawatani still lay in a deep sleep. Cankuwasté asked another man to stay with the boy, while he and Bear Walker joined others at the sweat lodge for an inipi rite. Talks With Owls joined them.

At the end of the first part of the ceremony, the helper outside the initi passed the pipe inside to Talks with Owls. The men each took a drink of water to replenish their bodies. The pipe was offered to the four directions, Grandmother Earth and Grandfather Sky. After sharing the pipe, it was returned to the helper. Talks With Owls prayed to Wakan Tanka to look upon them, asking for the knowledge to heal Mawatani.

Water was, again, placed on the hot stones. The steam was thick; the air heavy. The heady aroma of sage, sweetgrass and tobacco permeated the lodge.

As the men sat in meditation and prayer, sweat poured from their bodies, purifying them and making them strong. Talks With Owls started to chant softly and his body began to rock to the rhythms of his mind.

I think he is having a vision, Bear Walker thought. *I will ask Wakan Tanka to make his vision strong and clear.*

Several minutes had passed, when the chants of the old man became louder and he raised his hands to the heavens: "Hyo! Hyo! Hyo! Hyo! Pilamaya, Tunkasila; thank you for your goodness to our people. We walk the sacred Mother Earth in happiness and thanksgiving. May all generations walk upon Her in a sacred manner."

The men carried Mawatani to Talks With Owls' lodge, laid him in front of the old man, and sat in a circle. Talks With Owls made an announcement:

"The boy is well. I have seen it."
"Hyaa-a-a-a," the men all repeated. This was good news.
"What have you seen?" Bear Walker asked.

Looking straight ahead, Talks With Owls closed his eyes, recapturing the vision in his mind. He then recounted what he had seen.

"I have seen, in the distance, a young man, lame, but strong of heart and mind. The distance was so great I was unable to see clearly, but by his side, some form of four-legged person sat, and a winged person circled above him. As I studied this for a while, the face of the young man suddenly filled the vision. I saw it was Mawatani, grown in wisdom and stature. The boy is not ill. He is in a vision trance. He will share this vision with me, and I will study it."

"Hyaa-a-a-a!" the men repeated. They were thankful for this vision, and pleased the boy was well. They were always grateful for visions that helped their people.

Chapter 12

· ·

The Dawning Of Wisdom

It was not until the late afternoon of the second day that Mawatani woke. Yawning and stretching, he was surprised his body felt so stiff; even more than usual. He lay stretching his back, flexing his shoulders and extending his legs. A smile formed as he thought of how much he must look like his dog that always made a production out of stretching when he first awoke.

He became aware of the strong odor of kinnickinnick. Yawning again, he painfully turned on his back. Slowly, his eyelids strained to lift. When they were about half open, he realized he was not in his own lodge. The last time this happened, it was Singing Lark he saw when he awoke. *Now where am I, and why?*

Mawatani sat up, attempting to orient himself. He turned and saw Talks With Owls. Three other men, including Bear Walker, sat in a circle inside of the lodge.

Mawatani was so perplexed he didn't know what to say. "What am I doing here?" he asked. "Where is my family?"

He quickly looked himself over to see if he was injured again. He seemed to be fine. Looking at Bear Walker, he asked, "Why am I here? Is something wrong?"

"There is nothing wrong, Mawatani," Talks With Owls replied. "Have you had a vision?"

"A vision?" *Yes,* he thought. *I did have a vision. It was very real and clear, but little happened in it.* "Yes. I had a vision. How did you know?"

"There were signs," the old man answered. "We must talk about this vision. Visions are the dawning of wisdom."

"Yes, but there is little to tell," the boy said. "The vision was very uneventful. It only lasted a short time."

"You will tell me about this uneventful vision. It might tell us much," replied Talks With Owls.

"Why am I not in my own lodge with my family?"

"We were unable to wake you yesterday morning," Bear Walker said. "At first we thought you were ill, or that the evil spirits had entered your body. Cankuwasté was unable to wake you, so we brought you to Talks With Owls. He told us you were having a vision."

"I have been sleeping for a whole day?" Mawatani asked.

"You have been sleeping for almost two days," Talks With Owls said.

"You were taken to the lodge of Cankuwasté the first morning. Your mother was frightened."

Mawatani sat in disbelief. "Two days? I must let her know I am well."

"You will go to her," the old man said. "First, we will talk."

Mawatani thought about the meaning of this two-day sleep. *I'm sure the vision did not last for more than a few moments. How can such an insignificant vision take two days and have important meaning? If it had been a powerful vision and taken two days, I could understand it. I have heard of that happening*

78

*before. How disappointing to have taken two days to
have had such a meager one.*

The men went to their lodges, leaving Talks With
Owls alone with Mawatani.

Talks With owls instructed Mawatani to reflect
on his vision and keep it fresh in his mind. Before
sending him home to his family, he asked him to
return soon. He would then ask him to share his
vision.

"Then my visions are real," Mawatani thought out
loud.

"Ah," the old man said, "You have had other
visions?"

"I...I guess so," Mawatani stammered.

"Then yes, I believe your visions are real. The
Great Spirit is beckoning to you. You must answer his
call. We will work together to help you understand
these visions."

Mawatani lost no time getting to his lodge. He
was hungrier than he ever remembered being. He
had not seen his family for two days. As he neared
the tipi, the enticing aroma of his mother's cooking
made him quicken his pace. As anxious as he was
to see them, he entered his home calmly, as though
he had been out playing with his friends. Holy Moon
Woman's eyes lit up with relief when he entered.
Takcawe beamed with sisterly love.

Mawatani gave Capa Winhaha a loving tap on his
shoulder and picked up Comes Alone, holding him
high. "Hau, misunkala. Has my little brother behaved
well for his mother and sister today?"

Comes Alone giggled and began to cry in protest
when Mawatani put him back in his cradleboard.
Mawatani pinched his nose as a reminder that crying
was not acceptable.

Over the ages, his people found if they pinched the nose of a crying baby, it would force them to stop. For centuries, this was the way it was done. From the time of birth, this practice is used. Babies seldom cried after they were a few months old. Crying babies could bring death to the whole tiyospaye if the enemy was near.

Comes Alone quickly stopped crying, but his closed lips puffed, his eyes watered and his upper body still trembled in silent protest. He loved when his big brother played with him, and he didn't want him to stop. A playful and loving fist to the chin from Mawatani seemed to suffice. A smile returned to his chubby face.

Looking at his mother and sister, Mawatani, again, had the urge to hold each of them in an embrace. He knew how worried his mother must have been, and a young girl learns from her mother. Going to Takcawe', he laid his hand on her shoulder. Turning to his mother, he gently placed his hand on her cheek. Though he said nothing, his eyes spoke his thoughts to her.

After dinner, Mawatani went to the lodges of Six Toes and Catches Tail. Together, they went to a secluded area beneath the cottonwoods, next to the creek. Unseen, Etonka followed them, hiding behind a clump of bushes. He strained to hear what the boys were saying.

Mawatani did not share the contents of his vision, but let his friends know that he believed a dream that took two days must be a sign, no matter how uneventful and, seemingly short, it was. He would be spending much of his time with Talks With Owls in an attempt to learn what message he should learn from this sign.

The two boys were not used to this introspective side of their friend. There was one thing of which they were certain; Mawatani was serious. This probably meant that he would soon be preparing for his first hanbleceya, his first vision quest. This was the first real step toward manhood. They were excited for their friend. Putting their outstretched hands on Mawatani's shoulders, they pledged an unspoken promise to stand by him during this time.

Etonka approached the boys. "So, Mawatani is going to prepare for his hanbleceya. He will find that is not an easy task. I know. I have now spent time on two hanbleceyas and nothing happened either time. Nothing! Mawatani does not have the spirit or the strength to cry for a vision. The crying part, he can do. But he is not man enough to have a real vision."

Catches Tail looked at Etonka. "Go away, Etonka."

"No. Wait, Matoska." Mawatani tried to get him to stop. "Wait, please." Etonka ran from them.

"There is nothing you can do about him, Mawatani. Give it up. He is hopeless," Six Toes said in disgust.

"I don't believe that," replied Mawatani.

The boys sat in silence.

Mawatani thought of his new friend, Zicahota. *I will go to him soon and ask him to be with me during this time. He will listen well to my thoughts and be a good companion.* After a few moments more with his friends, he bid them goodnight and returned to his lodge. There was so much to think about.

Chapter 13

The Blossoming Of Friendship

Sleep came only in spurts during the night. Mawatani lay, eyes open, staring into the darkness. During the many waking moments, he reflected on the best way to begin this spiritual journey upon which he was about to embark. He had now made a decision.

He was looking forward to his time with Talks With Owls, but there was one thing he wanted to do first. *I will go to Zicahota. It is important that he know about my vision. I want him to be a part of this journey. I will tell him of my silent and uninspiring vision.*

Mawatani was unable to understand why he felt the need to share this special time with Zicahota; after all, he hardly knew him. There was something about this new friend; something that energized him. His character was strong. His commitment to who he is was firm. That strength and commitment was something he needed right now. There was a connection with Zicahota that did not exist with his old friends. It was more serious; more grown-up. Whatever it was, he sensed it was important to him; very important.

Mawatani stood quietly, clumsily shaking his bad leg to loosen the stiffness. He picked up his bow, placed a few pieces of pemmican in a small pouch, and left his lodge. A tenuous outline of the horizon was appearing as he stepped outside and walked towards his uncle's lodge.

Bear Walker woke quickly when Mawatani's hand touched his shoulder. When Mawatani told him of his plan, his uncle agreed that sharing this time with Zicahota would be good. "The boy has a strong heart. He will be a good helper."

As Mawatani stepped outside, he turned back to Bear Walker. "Tell my mother I have gone to see my friend. I will return in three sleeps. Tell Talks With Owls I will see him when I return. This is something I must do."

It was early afternoon when Night Eagle's camp came into view. Mawatani made good time. Napasni did not even break into a sweat.

A lookout saw him and announced his coming. Several people left their work to come and welcome him. As he greeted them, he scanned the village looking for Zicahota.

Ah, I should have known, Mawatani thought. *There he is, standing at the back of the others, as usual.* He slipped off Napasni and led him toward his friend. To his embarrassment, small children surrounded him, asking to hear his story again.

"Perhaps later," he told the children. "Now, I must speak with Zicahota." With that, the children happily began to disperse, yelling "Don't forget." "We'll remind you." They made it obvious that he would not be able to leave until the story was told.

When he reached his friend, they placed an arm on each other's shoulders in greeting.

"I must speak with you, kola," Mawatani said.

"We'll go by the creek, Bear Killer." Zicahota did not wait for Mawatani's approval. He turned and walked towards the water.

The creek was calm, splashing tranquilly on the rocks. The water flowed gently on its passage toward its convergence with some other body of water where it would increase in volume and strength.

At first, the boys just sat; Zicahota on a stump and Mawatani on a large, flat rock. Nothing was said for a while. The boys took in the sounds and the message of the creek.

"You can learn much from the waters of the creek," Mawatani finally said. "It does not let small things stop its journey. It goes over, under, or around these obstacles to get where it is going. Unless it is forced to stop by a dam, it lets nothing stop it, even if it is something large. It just continues towards its goal."

"You sound like a wise old man," Zicahota said, continuing to stare at the creek, "but what you say is true. I have never thought about it before."

"The water's goal is never really met, because it changes as it continues its journey," Mawatani continued, "It gains strength from where it has been, becoming more sure of where it is going."

Zicahota turned to his friend. "Your thoughts are deep, kola. Before you have even experienced your first hanbleceya, you sound like a wise old wicasa wakan. Why do you tell me these things?"

"It should be the same with us, Zicahota," Mawatani answered. "I allowed twelve moons to pass, trapped by a dam I built myself. I didn't try to pass over or under it. I spent so much time feeling sorry for myself I left no time to find a path around it. The waters of my life did not flow and gain strength from my journey. They receded, leaving little islands of myself with no connection to the life the Great Spirit has given me."

Zicahota rose and went to Mawatani, his eyes full of wonder. "These are very wise things you are saying, Bear Killer, but why do you say them to me? Have you spoken of these things with Talks With Owls or have you come to speak with Hears The Voice?"

"Niye kici wawaglaka wacin ye," replied Mawatani. "I came to speak with you. Kola, I had a vision. Talks With Owls knows this and we will talk when I return. He will help me break the dam I built and prepare me for my hanbleceya. When that time comes, I want you to be there as one of my helpers. I want you to share the inipi and be nearby when I go to the mountain."

"I will be there," Zicahota, answered. "I am honored that you have asked me to share in this." The two boys were inseparable the rest of the day.

That evening, while eating at the lodge of Zicahota's family, Mawatani finally met his friend's sister, Kimimila. It was she, he was told, who thought he was the finest looking hokshila within the Paha Sapa.

Kimimila was about the age of Tahcawé, but she flirted openly for his attention, which embarrassed him. More than that, it made him wonder if Takcawe might also be flirting with the boys in their camp. He hadn't noticed that she was, but he would start paying more attention when he returned. An older brother must protect his sister from the advances of the local young men. *She is still so young,* he thought.

Later, Mawatani visited with Hears The Voice and Singing Lark. He then went to the lodge of Night Eagle, sharing news of his village.

Mawatani spoke of how well Bear Walker was healing and how thankful he was for the help he received from Night Eagle's tiyospaye.

With both villages low on fresh meat and skins, men from each village joined to seek out where the buffalo were grazing now.

"The herd should return soon," Night Eagle said. "The heavy rains left some time ago and Mother Earth has swallowed most of the excess water."

After their visit, Mawatani returned to the lodge of Zicahota's family, where they talked for a while, then bedded down for the night.

Early morning came and the night had been restful. The day lay before the two boys. As they left the lodge, Zicahota said, "Let's go back to the creek."

With bows and arrows in hand, the boys walked to the creek, where Zicahota showed Mawatani new arrows he had made. Setting targets, he demonstrated their quality and his skill by hitting every target with accuracy Mawatani had never seen.

"It is not the arrows, Mawatani. They are nothing special. It is the bow of your father. I feel his spirit within it. I talk to his spirit, and my skill has improved with his guidance."

After the demonstration was over, the two sat by the creek in thought and conversation.

"Do you ever want to go to a place away from others?" Mawatani asked, "a place where there will be no other two-leggeds, just to be alone with your thoughts? I don't mean like a hanbleceya, but just alone?"

"Yes, I do it often."

"What is it like?"

"For me, it sustains my life. I want only good things for my people. I will do what I am able to contribute to them, but I am not comfortable around others as you are. Unlike you, I am not a teller of stories or a companion to small children. It is when I am alone I gather strength and courage."

"I receive much strength from others," Mawatani said, "but there are times when I feel a great need to find a quiet place; a place where I can examine myself and reflect on the path the Great Spirit has in mind for me."

"I know of such a place, and spend much time there," Zicahota replied.

"It must be wonderful," Mawatani said.

"For me, it brings purpose to my life," Zicahota answered. "Come, we will get our horses and I'll take you there."

Jumping on their horses, the boys headed toward the Makosica, the Badlands.

The sun was leaving the western horizon when they returned. After their evening meal, Mawatani joined the children who had been waiting for his story. As he sat amongst them, he wondered how Zicahota could feel uncomfortable being around them. They were so open to your word; so honest in their responses.

His story told, Mawatani left the youngsters with this thought: "It is good to hear the stories of the deeds of others. It is best to use these stories as guides to aid you in following your own paths and living your own stories. Whatever path you choose, it must be one that will be of most benefit to our people."

As he left the children, he wondered how he could say these things when he didn't even know his own path yet.

Early the next morning, Mawatani said his goodbyes and began his journey home. As he galloped away, the coat of Napasni glistened in the early light of dawn.

Chapter 14

The Visions Merge

Mawatani woke refreshed and full of anticipation the next morning. He quickly dressed and hurried to the lodge of his uncle. Bear Walker wanted to walk with him as he went to meet with Talks With Owls.

As they walked, Mawatani stopped. "Até, perhaps I should tell you about my vision first."

"No, Mawatani," Bear Walker answered. "I am looking forward to learning about it, but you must tell Talks With Owls first. He will know better how to respond to what you tell him."

"It is not much of a vision, uncle, maybe not even worth telling. I am almost embarrassed to tell it to such a wise and holy man as Talks With Owls."

"No, Mawatani. He too, had a vision during your long sleep. It was about you, and is how he knew you were not ill, but were having a vision. Perhaps he will tell you what he saw."

Mawatani was amazed. "Talks With Owls had a vision about me?"

"Yes, and every vision has meaning, a message. There is a reason you were given this vision. Talks With Owls is very wise and will understand its meaning. His counsel will help to set you on a path to travel on your journey to manhood. I will hear your story after you have shared it with him."

Reaching Talks With Owls lodge, Bear Walker placed his hands on his nephew's shoulders. "While you are with this wise old man, listen carefully to what he tells you. Hear what he says, and what he does not say. Open your heart and your mind to all these things. When he asks a question, pick your words carefully. Say only those things that must be said. This will help him understand the message. I take great pride in you, Mawatani. I am proud to call you my son. This is truly the dawn of a new day for you." He returned to his lodge and family.

Mawatani suddenly felt alone, self-conscious and apprehensive. His excitement and great eagerness to understand himself, allowed him to make his presence known.

"Talks With Owls, it is me, Mawatani."

"Ah, that is good," the boy heard. "Enter."

Taking in a deep breath, Mawatani slowly stepped inside. The aroma of burning sage filled the lodge. Talks With Owls was sitting, facing the East. He motioned for the boy to sit across from him.

The old man said nothing at first. He sat, eyes closed, body rocking ever so slightly. Mawatani stared at him, wondering what thoughts and prayers went through the mind of the holy man. He knew that Talks With Owls came by his name for good reason. It was known he was able to talk with the owl, the wisest of all the winged people. Because of this, he had a messenger who would take his messages directly to the sky spirits. *What did he learn from them?*

Pondering all these things, he was deep in thought when the old man's voice suddenly reverberated in chant. Mawatani was so startled, his body jumped in surprise and his heart began to pound. It took a while for his heart to return to its normal rhythm.

When calm returned, the old man was still intoning, sending his voice to the Great Mystery.

Mawatani wondered if he would ever be allowed to tell his vision. Silently, his hands began to tap out the rhythm of the old man's chant on his legs. Soon, his body began to move to the pattern of his hands. Leaning forward, he looked directly at the old man's closed eyes, wondering if they would ever open.

As suddenly as it started, the chanting ceased. Mawatani sat straight up, not wanting to be caught staring.

Talks With Owls picked up a bundle lying at his side. Slowly, he opened the skin bag and Mawatani saw it was the old man's channunpa, his sacred pipe. *Oh,* Mawatani thought, *he will smoke his pipe first. This will further delay my telling of the vision.*

Reverently, the old man fit the pipe stem to the bowl. Laying the pipe on his lap, he took a braid of sweetgrass and laid it on the fire. The fragrant aroma of the burning grass mixed with the heady scent of sage. Mawatani's attention began to focus on the fire.

Leaning over the fire, and slightly cupping his hands, Talks With Owls directed the smoke over his face, around his head, and continued until his entire body was blessed by the sacred smoke. He motioned for the boy to bless himself in the same manner.

Mawatani began to copy the old man's gestures, bringing the smoke first to his face. As it reached his nostrils, his heart seemed to expand. He had done this many times, but, for the first time, he actually felt the true sacredness of what he was doing. It was exciting. It was amazing. His breathing increased, coming in short but heavy spurts. His hands, almost frenzied, kept reaching for more of the smoke, as he directed it towards his body as though intoxicated by it. He then experienced something he had never felt before. It wasn't really a feeling. It was more of an awareness; an exhilaration. It was a sense of a part of him he didn't know; a part he could not identify. He knew that Tunkasila, the creator, was there with him.

Being so involved in what was taking place within him, he didn't notice that Talks With Owls had placed his hands over the fire, motioning for him to complete the ritual. Quickly, Mawatani sat up, his mind reeling from what had taken place. Looking into the eyes of the holy man with such powerful medicine, he wondered how he would ever be able to explain all these feelings to him.

He saw that Talks With Owls' eyes were also on him, but his gaze was different. *It is as though he can see right into me and understand the frenzy of my mind*, Mawatani thought. He felt comforted by the old man's eyes. *I am seeing Talks With Owls in a different way*, he thought. *His eyes are full of wisdom and understanding. There is safety with this old man.* He began to relax.

Talks With Owls began to fill his pipe. He picked up a bag of kinnickinnick, a mixture of tobacco, sweet grass, bearberries, and shavings of tree bark. He took a pinch of it, passing it through the smoke from the sweetgrass before placing it in the pipe. He then took another, and another, each time, purifying it over the smoke.

Why is he taking so long? Mawatani wondered. *Will the telling of my vision ever happen?*

With the pipe filled, the old man rose; his old bones still amazingly agile. Holding the stem of the pipe upward, he invoked Grandfather, the Sky. He then raised it to the spirits of the East, South, West, and North. Finally, he held the stem toward

91

the ground to honor Grandmother, the Earth. After making these offerings, he sat and took three puffs.

Mawatani watched all this carefully. He had seen this ceremony many times, but had never been a part of it. Thinking it was finally time to tell his story, he took a deep breath, closed his eyes, and began to focus on what he would say.

Feeling ready, he opened his eyes. What he saw caused him to quickly close them again. *Did I really see it? Is it possible?*

Reopening his eyes, Mawatani saw it was real. Talks With Owls was offering him the pipe.

"Hau, Até, Mawatani," the old man said.

"You are offering the pipe to me?" Mawatani asked.

"This time is holy, Mawatani. You and I are to share your vision. We need the powers of the four directions and of Grandmother and Grandfather to help us interpret this message you have received. Here, take the pipe and smoke it. From it, you will draw strength and insight from the powers which I have placed there."

"I have not proven myself in battle," Mawatani said. "I have not earned this honor."

"Ah, but you have, grandson. In saving Bear Walker, you showed you are alert to the needs of others. You endured much pain and showed great courage when you killed the bear. Even after doing these things, you did not falter. You were willing to sacrifice your life to save Bear Walker, and you performed with bravery in killing the bear. You showed perseverance in all you did to find help from others. These are the things that show me that you have earned this honor."

After sitting wide-eyed, looking from the pipe to Talks With Owls and back to the pipe again, Mawatani said, "Hau, Tunkashila," took the pipe, handling it as if it might break. He brought the stem to his mouth. His mind was so full; a jumble of swirling thoughts.

His thoughts turned to what he was about to do. *Unpa. I am to smoke the pipe. This is something that will never happen to me again. Only once can you do something for the first time.*

Mawatani closed his eyes to focus on the moment. Opening his eyes, he took a deep breath, then a puff from the pipe.

His first thought was not as holy as he had hoped. He quickly learned that kinnickinnick tastes much stronger than it smells. After a short pause, he cautiously took two more quick puffs, and returned the pipe to Talks With Owls. Never had Wakan Tanka felt so real; so near; so much a part of who he was.

"You did well, Mawatani," Talks With Owls said. "I could see that you put much thought into what you were doing. My decision to share the pipe with you was a good one." Smoking the pipe until the tobacco was gone, Talks With Owls sat it next to him, leaning it against a rock.

"Now," Talks With Owls said, "before you tell me of your vision, do you understand this pipe ceremony we just shared? Do you know why we offer it to the four directions and to Grandfather and Grandmother?"

Mawatani was still rather breathless, partly from the kinnickinnick, but mostly from the emotional high he felt from sharing the pipe for the first time.

"Yes, Grandfather. My até and Bear Walker spent many hours telling me stories of Tatanka Pte Ska, who was White Buffalo Woman. They told me how she brought the pipe to us and told us how to use it. From the time I was small, they taught me about the four directions and of Grandmother Earth and Grandfather Sky.

"Offering the pipe to the East is a tribute to Wakan Tanka. From this direction we are given light, which is knowledge. Next, it is offered to the South, which is the giver of life. The pipe is offered to the West because it is where the sun goes down and is the home of the winged power. It is offered to the North because that is where the giant, Waziya lives. He causes the winds to help purify our land and gives us breath so we may live."

"What else did they teach you," the old man asked.

"Many things," Mawatani replied. "First, he taught me about the medicine wheel, and how each direction of the wheel represents a part of our lives we must develop in order to be complete. Being complete allows us to live in peace and tranquility.

"My até told me about the creation of the two-leggeds, the four-leggeds and the winged people. He taught me about the spirit world and the guardians of the good red road. This is the road going North and South, which stands for purity. He told of the blue road that runs East and West; the road of error and destruction. People who travel this road think more of themselves than of the people."

The old man nodded. "Your father and uncle taught you well. Now, tell me, Mawatani, was this your first vision?"

"No, grandfather. I have had many visions; visions which were greater and more exciting. They just didn't take as long as this one."

"Tell me of these visions."

Mawatani sighed. *When is he going to let me talk about the vision that took two days and where nothing happened?* Sighing again, he began to tell of his earlier visions. He was almost afraid to tell him how thunder was almost always a part of them, but he did. Then he told of how a sungmanitu, the sacred wolf, began to enter into them.

Mawatani paused before continuing. *Should I tell him how I began to interpret these visions after my father died: how I believed the thunder of my earlier visions represented how my father would die, and the ones after were from spirits who wanted to taunt me, continually reminding me?*

Bear Walker's last words before he left him this morning, entered his mind. Choose your words carefully. It will help the holy man interpret your vision. Mawatani decided to tell the old man these thoughts and his earlier visions.

"Ahh," Talks With Owls exclaimed when the boy finished. He then began to chant, thanking the Great Spirit for the boy's visions.

Again, Mawatani's body jumped in surprise, not expecting a prayer of thanks for his faulty thinking.

Talks With Owls' chanting stopped, but he sat in silence, eyes closed.

Mawatani was about to burst. *When is he going to let me share my new vision?* He tried to enter into the old man's prayerful silence, but his own thoughts were too noisy.

Finally, the old man opened his eyes. After a moment, he took the pipe and refilled it. Once again, he stood and offered it to the four directions, Grandfather Sky and Grandmother Earth. After sitting, he lifted the stem to his mouth, took three puffs and handed it to Mawatani.

Mawatani's impatience disappeared, as he too, took three puffs and returned the sacred pipe to Talks With Owl. It was then returned to the rock.

"We will talk more of these things in the days to come, but now, tell me of this latest vision."

95

Finally, thought Mawatani. *Now if there was only something exciting to tell him.*

"There is little to tell, Grandfather. I sat on a rock, in thought. Soon a sungmanitu, the sacred wolf, appeared, and he too, did nothing. He sat looking at me, his eyes like liquid; dark and bright. He remained there, not moving, just staring. It seemed this would last forever. Then, just before I woke, an owl flew down from a mountain and landed on the back of the wolf. For the first time, the sungmanitu turned his eyes away from me to look at the owl.

The two of them stared at each other for a moment, then both turned to look at me again. Suddenly, they disappeared. They didn't run or fly away; they just disappeared."

Mawatani told all there was to tell.

Talks With Owls sat in silence. His face showed just the hint of a smile. He again, picked up the pipe, filled it, and offered it up.

"Hyaa-a-a, Hyaa-a-a, Hyaa-a-a, Hyaa-a-a." Raising the pipe to Grandfather, the sky, he prayed;

> "O Great Spirit,
> You who knows us better than any other;
> You, who gives us the light of knowledge and truth;
> I have placed each of the powers in this sacred pipe to honor them and ask them to join us in this boy's journey into manhood.
> We ask for your help in this because you know all things. Help me understand this powerful vision you have given this young man so I may lead him upon the good red path."

How can he call this a powerful vision? Mawatani thought. *Nothing happened.*

Talks With Owls told Mawatani of the vision he had during the time of his long sleep. The vision was of a young man, lame, but strong of heart and mind. He stood proudly; a four-legged at his side and a winged person circling above.

"The young man was you, Mawatani, in a future time," the old man said. "The four-legged was your wolf. The four-legged I saw was the spirit of your wolf. The winged person I saw was your owl. Our visions are one. The Great Spirit has given us each a simple melody but has played it for us in a different manner.

"In your vision, the melody is strong and clear. In mine, it was more of a suggestion; a tune which I could not grasp, yet it had a lingering melody that would not leave me. We will talk in the days to come and learn more of this melody. There will be other melodies. We will learn how to put them together to make your song of life.

"This journey will be long, but we will take it together. It is the road that has been given to us. We must learn how to follow it. Be attentive to your dreams, Mawatani. They will help us as we walk this road together."

PART IV
THE PREPARATION

Chapter 15

The Crooked Path

Preparation for the Wiwanyank Wacipi, the sacred sun dance, was in progress. Bear Walker was chosen as this year's leader. Finding a place to hold the ceremony was his first task. Night Eagle's tiyospaye would be joining them, so a larger area was needed.

Supplying ample food was a concern this year. Without the buffalo, the only fresh meats to be found in the area were antelope, deer and occasional prairie hens. All the villages in the area were in the same fix.

The flood waters were finally absorbed, the dried grass had been burned off the grazing grounds, and the rain had encouraged abundant new grasses. Still, there were no buffalo.

Even though preparations for the Sun Dance had been in progress for several days, men were sent out to search for signs of the great herd. The need for meat was great, but the need for hides, fat, thread and glue was even greater. The buffalo gave them all these things. If they returned, the Sun Dance would have to wait.

Several days passed since Mawatani's first meeting with Talks With Owls. Everyday life in the village continued in its busy patterns, along with preparation for the Sun Dance, but he was not a part of it. His life was now consumed with the telling and retelling of his visions and learning the stories of their people.

He was learning about the Seven Council Fires and the seven ceremonies of their nation. The many stories of his people, their history and their legends, were becoming a part of who he was. His understanding of who his people were, where they had been, and who they strived to be, was much clearer now. He was excited about learning more.

"All these things that make up the Tree of Knowledge come from Mother Earth. They are what we earth people are meant to learn," Talks With Owls told him. "The Tree of Life comes only with walking the good red road and leading a good and spiritual life. As long as you stay on this path, knowledge will bloom, and the people will prosper. Follow the blue road, the path of material things, and the tree will wither and die. All these things must be learned."

At first, Mawatani could hardly wait to get to Talks With Owls' lodge each morning. The two were almost inseparable.

Mawatani loved hearing the legends of his people. He had learned many of them from his father, but he never tired of hearing them again.

Now, Talks With Owls was telling of Waziya and Wakanaka, and their daughter, Ité. He heard how Ité became enchanted by Tate, the Wind, and of their quadruplet sons. The story, as the old man told it, took several hours, as there were many more relatives and acquaintances who seemed to constantly misbehave.

"You must become acquainted with all the gods," Talks With Owls told Mawatani, "so you may call upon them."

For several days, the old man concentrated on Tobtob Kin, the Four-Times-Four Gods, who were the good gods.

Over the weeks, Mawatani took in the stories of Wikin, the Sun; Hanwikin, the Night Sun, and Takuskanskan, the god of all that moved, He learned of Tatekin, Tob kin, the Four Winds, Yumnikin, the Whirlwind, Makakin, the Earth, and Inyankin, the Rock.

Mawatani's head was spinning but Talks With Owls continued,

"I know this is difficult, Mawatani. Most young men do not learn all these things. They are taught enough by their fathers or uncles to have a successful hanbleceya, and learn the rest with age. You have a special gift. It is important to take full advantage of it. Knowing our stories will help you understand your visions.

"You must learn more about Tatankakan, the Buffalo Bull, Hunanpakan, the Two-legged Grizzly Bear; Wanagi, the Human Spirit; Waniya, Human Life; Nagila, the non-human Spirits, and Wasicunpi, the Guardian Spirits."

There is so much to learn, Mawatani thought.

Talks With Owls then told of the bad gods; Iyo, Gnaskinyan, the Crazy Buffalo. Then there was Anog Ite, Mini Watu, Ungla,

Gica, and many others.

Mawatani felt that his head would burst. *How am I ever going to remember all these things?*

Talks With Owls continually spoke of the importance of the inipi ceremony.

"It is during the inipi where the life of your body, the ni, is made strong and the body is purified. The ni is what you breathe and what comes into your body. The sweating of the body is what purifies it.

The ni comes into you at birth. It is the breath of life. If your ni leaves the body, you die.

"Making steam with the spirit of the water and hot rocks cleanses the inside of your body and makes it strong. This is called ini. The temni, the water that comes from the body, are the impurities the bad spirits continually try to place within us. The inipi is the only way to combat those impurities and cleanse the inside of our bodies.

"Because of its importance, the initi, or sweat lodge, must be built in a sacred manner. The initi must be kept closed because that is how the spirit of the water is held, and we are able to breathe it into our bodies."

The more Mawatani learned about himself and his people, the more he realized how little he knew and understood before his time with Talks With Owls. This would be a long journey; one that would never end.

One day, Talks With Owls began talking about Mawatani's future leadership responsibilities. At first, it pleased him and gave his self-image a boost. The more he thought about what it meant, the more uncomfortable he became with it.

"You will become a great leader, Mawatani," the old man said. "Wakan Tanka has given you a great gift. This gift was given to you because you have suffered much. No one can achieve greatness without suffering."

Talks With Owls continued: "You must continue to study all the lessons of the wisdom, the knowledge, the power and the gift of the medicine wheel. Everything you do or think, do to strengthen your understanding of the four directions of this wheel. This will enable you to bring good medicine to our people. Your counsel will be sought after and welcomed by many."

The more Mawatani reflected on these words, the more anxiety he felt. They even frightened him. *How can this be true? Only a short time ago I had no life. My actions towards myself, my family, and my people were shameful; completely lacking in virtue. How is it now, that I am wise and on a path to greatness? I am not sure that I want this greatness.*

Talks With Owls spent time preparing Mawatani to take part in the upcoming Wiwanyank Wacipi, the dance looking at the Sun. Talks With Owls chose him to be the one to give the final strike of the ax to the sacred cottonwood tree chosen to serve as the canwakan, the center pole of the sun dance. This honor was usually given to a respected member of the village; one who lived a good and holy life.

Mawatani's thoughts remained focused on the last year; a year of waste, when he accepted no responsibilities. He did nothing for himself or his tiyspaye. *Is there nothing between this and expectations of greatness? Can't I just be a good brave who helps in hunting the buffalo and protecting my family and my people? Perhaps Talks With Owls is mistaken. Maybe I left something out of my story; something that would change its meaning.*

At night he stayed awake, reflecting on these things, but decided nothing was left unsaid. Nothing he had said was not as he had seen and understood it.

Mawatani felt overwhelmed. He no longer lived with happy anticipation of his time with Talks With Owls. His visits continued, but the time he spent with him grew less and less. He began to feel as though he was trapped when he was with him. It was as though life, itself, was crowding him into a place that was too small; a place from which there was no escape.

No longer would he visit the old man's lodge. He needed time away from him; time to live as his friends lived; time to just be a part of the village. He no longer wanted to be a young boy wasting his childhood being prepared for greatness. *I wasted enough time last year,* he thought. *This year I will grow and mature like Six Toes and Catches Tail. Talks with Owls can pick someone else to cut down the sacred tree. There are many here who deserve the honor more than I do.*

Chapter 16

. . . .

The Fickle Mind

For the next few days, Mawatani spent his time freely, catching up with his life. He finished the new bow he started before his visits with Talks With Owls. He honed his skills, chipping new arrowheads with his friends. This was the freedom he longed for.

One day he asked Catches Tail and Six Toes to join him, as he tested his new bow. Bows and arrows in hand, the three walked along the creek, away from the camp.

As the boys reached a bend in the creek, Catches Tail said, "Let's stop here. This is a good place to play 'see who shoots the farthest'."

The other two agreed, seeing there was a natural clearing where nothing would interfere with the path of the arrows.

Six Toes began to boast. "My arrows will go the farthest. My bow is made from the finest wood I have ever seen. I climbed high into a beautiful ash tree to cu t just the right limb."

"We'll see," countered Catches Tail. "My arrows are made from chokecherry. I'll give you three of my best arrowheads if my arrows do not fall beyond yours."

"You have lost three arrowheads, kola," Six Toes responded with a smile.

Mawatani was timid about his boast. "This bow is new and untried, but my craftsmanship will bear your boasts."

When the contest got underway, Mawatani's claim proved accurate. His new bow did well, meeting, and twice exceeding, the distances of his friends. Catches Tail did not lose any arrowheads. He was the overall winner of the game.

"Someday we will have Zicahota join us," Mawatani suggested. "He is the best I have ever seen. He is even better than the best brave in his village. We can learn much from him."

"Sure, Mawatani," Catches Tail answered quietly. "Someday we will do that. There are probably a few things he could learn from us, too."

Mawatani recognized the tone of his voice and heard what he did not say. *Perhaps I do speak of Zicahota too much*, he thought. *If they only understood our friendship, they would see that it does nothing to lessen my friendship with them. It is a different kind of friendship; more like a relationship between men. Anyway, it is important to me right now.* He quickly changed the subject.

The boys walked away from the creek to retrieve their arrows and returned to stroll along the creek bed.

Six Toes suddenly stopped, motioning for the others to do the same.

"Look," he said, pointing upstream... "hehaka."

Standing at the water's edge, drinking, were two large elks.

"They will feed many people," Mawatani whispered.

Each of the boys readied an arrow to his bow.

"O sacred elk," Mawatani whispered, "Forgive us for what we are about to do, but you have been sent to feed our people."

Again, Mawatani whispered. "Our arrows must be sure and straight. Catches Tail, you take the one nearest the water. I'll shoot the other one. Six Toes, you wait to see if another arrow is needed. If it is, shoot well. An injured four-legged will surely be on the run. I'll give the signal."

The three took aim and, on the signal, the first two arrows flew as one, downing one animal and badly injuring the other. Six Toes deftly dispatched his arrow, and the injured elk fell in its tracks.

The boys ran to the kill, whooping in celebration. They then thanked the elk for giving their lives to feed their people.

"We have no way to get this meat to the village," Mawatani said. "Catches Tail, you run the fastest. Go to the village and bring our horses. We will begin to butcher the meat."

Catches Tail raised his arms and yelled in celebration. "This time, we will bring in the meat." He ran toward the village, wearing a smile that wouldn't leave.

The boys soon discovered that skinning the animals, and keeping the hides as whole as possible, was not as easy as it looked. The women seemed to do it with no trouble at all.

Catches Tail returned with two pack horses and two women, who immediately took over the butchering. As happy as they were to have the meat, the women left no doubt in the boys' minds that the hide would be in much better condition if they had waited to let them do the skinning.

That evening, camped at the site of the Sun Dance, there was an informal gathering with people from Night Eagle's tiyospaye. The boys were acknowledged for their contribution.

As proud as he was to have contributed to the village, Mawatani was not feeling much like celebrating. It seemed wherever he went and whatever he did, the gaze of Talks With Owls followed him. As he ate, the old man sat across the circle. His stare was so intense Mawatani could feel it, as though a powerful ray of energy flowed from it.

Why does he stare at me? Mawatani thought. *Do I not have a right to read the direction of my own path?* Bear Walker told him the old man was still counting on him to down the tree. *Don't I have the right to decline this honor?*

Dancing began, and the drums sounded like the heartbeat of a nation. Mawatani hardly noticed. He had too many questions in his mind; questions that argued with the wisdom of his heart. No one but Talks With Owls noticed when he rose and rushed to his lodge. Only this wise old man saw him leave his lodge with a parfleche and bow & quiver in his hands. Only he saw Mawatani take Napasni from its tether and ride off to the north.

Chapter 17

The Escape

The warm night air rushed against Mawatani's face as he pushed Napasni to a gallop. It embraced him in welcome relief. He could breathe deeply and freely for the first time in days. Perhaps the best thing was, Talks With Owls was unable to constantly gaze at him. How grateful he was to Zicahota for showing him his special place for retreat. He needed such a place now.

Slowing the pace, he took in the marvelous peacefulness of the silence. His mind, free for the moment, became part of the only thing he could hear now; the rhythmic, nearly hypnotic cadence of Napasni's hoofs against the earth.

Soon, Mawatani realized he had not been directing the horse for some time and reined to a stop. In the moonlight, he looked for a landmark and smiled when he saw the silhouettes of the high-walled cliffs, the mounds, and the hundreds of spires and buttes that made up the Makosica.

He saw Cedar Butte to the Northeast, so he turned the horse, heading directly to it. From there, Napasni seemed to sense where they were going. He had been there many times before with Zicahota.

When he reached the area Zicahota showed him, the mountain hid the moon with such darkness he was unable to see the path to his friend's site. Tethering

Napasni to a dried bush, he found a sheltered spot next to some rocks. He built a fire and thanked Wakan Tanka for the solitude. He would wait until tomorrow to begin meditating on his future. He wanted nothing to break the peace he was feeling now. Listening to the sounds of the night, he fell asleep.

Mawatani awoke after the most restful sleep he had experienced in days. He chanted a short prayer to Tunkasila, thanking Him for the new day. Reaching into his parfleche, he pulled out a piece of pemmican, mounted Napasni, and rode toward Zicahota's private hideaway.

As he approached the path, he heard an eagle overhead. Watching it soar, he wondered at its beauty. *How freely it surveys the land and keeps watch over those of us confined to earth,* he thought. As he watched, the eagle swooped down to an area beyond where he could see. He went to see where it landed. Looking up, he found the bird sitting on a ledge high above a recess in the mountain. As he walked toward it, the eagle took flight. Mawatani watched it until it veered south and out of sight.

Returning to Napasni, Mawatani turned and looked again at the recess below where the eagle had landed. *This too, is a good place,* he thought. *Zicahota can keep his place private. This will be my own private place. After all, the eagle has shown it to me. It is meant to be.*

Mawatani studied the area, becoming familiar with the physical features it offered. At one edge of the recess, a large, narrow portion of mudstone protruded from the side of the mountain, curving to fashion a protective alcove; a perfect place to meditate. He liked this place even better than Zicahota's.

After preparing an altar, he burned sweetgrass, offering it to Wakan Tanka. He asked for assistance as he reflected on what to do with his life.

After prayer, he sat in silence trying to separate the many thoughts that lay tangled in his mind. "Wakan Tanka," he prayed, "please help me find the patience I will need to untangle these thoughts and calm the storm that rages within me."

By early afternoon, he thought his head would burst. The more he tried to gather his thoughts, the more they scattered. No matter how hard he tried to pick out a single thought to study its meaning, it seemed to liquefy and merge with all the others. It was like trying to separate one drop of water from the stream.

Suddenly, he stood, raised his arms to the sky, and let out a scream of frustration. Startled by the sudden sound, Napasni reared and tried to break free of his tether. Mawatani quickly went to his side and comforted him, apologizing for his outburst. He then mounted him, and they raced across the plains.

During his return to the alcove, late that afternoon, he passed several gorges and gullies. Some had an occasional plant, struggling to maintain life amidst little soil and less water. He was always amazed by the Makosica, with its dry, bald cliffs and spires in the midst of this expanse of grasses. He wondered again, why Grandmother Earth gave her people such a strange gift.

He slipped off Napasni and rubbed him down. The freedom he felt on the back of his stallion as they explored the plains, calmed him. The excitement of that freedom brought courage to continue his retreat.

I am going to have to stop running away every time things become difficult. I didn't run away from my uncle when the bear attacked. It is when my head gets so full and confused, I want to escape. It is these times that I am going to have to learn to control.

Sitting in his private alcove, he watched as the late afternoon shadows dissolved into dusk. A light rain had fallen, and when the night sun rose, its light caused the moist grass of the plains below to sparkle like a field of a million stars.

His frustrations continued the next day, with uncontrolled thoughts tumbling inside his head. He prayed, burned sweetgrass, and pleaded with the Spirit People to help him.

By afternoon, he was exhausted and hungry. He still had some pemmican, but decided to look for turnips and other roots. As he searched, he found a shelf in a nearby deep alcove that stored a small amount of water from the summer rains. Several plants attempted to grow there, some of them edible.

He ate, mounted Napasni, and left at a gallop. By the time he slowed the pace, the stallion was lathered and his breathing, labored. Mawatani was angry with himself for allowing this to happen. He had been enjoying the feelings of the wind in his face so much he forgot to remember the needs of his horse. He reined him in and dismounted.

"Napasni, forgive me for doing this to you. I wasn't thinking. I guess I still think more of my own needs than others. I'm sorry, kola."

After resting him for a while, he said to Napasni, "I'll take you to the creek where you can rest, and we can both quench our thirsts."

On their return from the creek, they passed an area of buttes that were so beautiful they almost took his breath away. The walls looked as if they were painted with layers of orange, green, red and silver. *Aah,* he thought, *this is the reason Grandmother gave us the Makosica; to remind us that there is beauty in everything if you look for it.*

Looking to the West, he saw great amounts of dust in the air. *The winds are acting strangely,* he thought.

The third morning began as the first two, with prayer and thought. He pleaded: "O Mitakuye Oyasin, I need the help of all my relations; the plants, the animals, the water, and the stone. When I return to my village, I will especially need the help of my people"

By midday he was finally able to organize and retrieve some of his thoughts and began to weave them into shapes and patterns he could discern.

Time went by quickly. Before long, the sun was well into the West, nearing the summits of the Paha Sapa.

Darkness came. The day was good, and his mind was much calmer now. His hunger brought him back to the alcove.

While eating, he began to look back on the things he had thought about today. He had so much to be thankful for; his friendships with Six Toes and Catches Tail, and the new and special friendship with Zicahota. There was the love for his family, the closeness he now felt to Bear Walker and his respect for Talks With Owls. The more he took inventory, the more he felt a love for his people.

That love was the primary thread of the thoughts he had unraveled. *If I truly love my people, I have a responsibility to them. If what Talks With Owls thinks is right, I must follow through on the spirit messages I receive from my visions.*

As he reached that point in his thoughts, his mind again turned to confusion. *I am not ready to become this leader. Why have I been chosen?*

115

Looking up, he scanned the skies and the millions of stars that were the Spirit People. Most of the stories of their people came from these Spirits; stories of courage and cowardice, kindness and selfishness, and right and wrong. These are the tales that have taught their people since they were placed on this earth. *I still have much to learn. My ignorance is the reason for my confusion. Talks With Owls is right. I will return for more of his wisdom. Only then can I decide what the spirits are telling me.*

There was another thing he realized while he was in isolation; he missed the people of his village. He missed the hustle and bustle of everyday life. He felt incomplete without it, unlike Zicahota, who needed little contact with others, and knew himself better in his solitude. *He is probably disappointed that I am not there for the Sun Dance. If anyone understands my need for solitude, it will be him.*

Thinking again of Zicahota, *How different we are, yet how drawn we are to each other. It is as though we have been given each other's friendship to keep a balance in our lives.*

After contemplating these thoughts, he grew tired and bedded down in the alcove. *I will spend one more day here piecing together all the wandering thoughts that have traveled through my head. This will help Talks With Owls when I share my stories with him.*

By late morning of the next day, he was amazed by how all of the disorganized bits and pieces of his brooding and reflection came together. They were more organized; little groups of thoughts he could think about or set aside.

By afternoon, he was so pleased with the calmness of his mind, he decided to spend one more day. He would not eat nor drink. He would spend the time in thankful prayer and fasting. It was only right that he offer this to the spirit people and to Wakan Tanka for the gift of this holy time.

When he awoke, the morning of the seventh day, the sun was already bright. Above, hawks and eagles; magpies and meadowlarks glided gracefully on the thermal breezes. He hadn't slept this late in years, but he was in no hurry. He offered his prayers and rode Napasni to the creek for water. For a while, he sat by the stream attempting to hear its message. *I believe it knows that I have enough messages in my mind right now. I have no room for new ones.*

In the early afternoon, he took some pemmican from his bundle, mounted Napasni, and began his trip home.

This time alone has been good, he thought. *It has allowed me to see many truths that others have been telling me. I owe my tiyospaye much. The more I learn, the more I will be able to serve my people. This is the reason for life in a tiyospaye: to serve the needs of each other.*

As late afternoon approached, Mawatani hurried their pace. He was anxious to find out how the Sun Dance went. He also wanted to apologize to Talks With Owls for not accepting the honor of downing the sacred tree.

As he neared the village, he became alarmed. There were no people; no tipis; no fires; no horses. *Where did they go?* Then, he remembered: *the men were looking for the buffalo. They must have found them. If I had been thinking, I would have known that the dust I saw the other day was from the buffalo.*

He found the tracks of many travois and footprints heading North. *I'll follow their tracks until dark. If I leave early in the morning I should be able to meet up with them by late afternoon.*

117

Before leaving, he thanked Wakan Tanka for bringing tatanka and the cows back.

The next morning, he continued to follow the tracks left by the travois. It was well into the afternoon that he saw Cedar Butte far off to the east. *I was much closer to them when I left my retreat,* he thought, as he made his way northwest. By late afternoon he crossed the Cheyenne River, South Fork Creek, and was nearing Red Shirt Creek. Still, there was no sign of the hunting party.

Rain began to fall, and the ground became slippery. Napasni was having trouble with his footing. Mawatani did not want to take a chance with him, so he found a sheltered area. *We will rest. I will wait until tomorrow to join them.*

Chapter 18

• •

The Hunt

Holy Moon Woman spoke with Bear Walker and Talks With Owls while the villagers were pulling up stakes and preparing to leave for the hunt. She did not want to join them until Mawatani returned. He had been away for four days now.

"He will feel abandoned, returning here to find no one."

"We will not leave you here alone," Bear Walker told her, "and the hunt is too important to us. You must travel with the others."

"He will be fine," Talks With Owls added. "Mawatani will find us."

"Of course he will," Bear Walker added. "He is a koskolaka. He does not need his mother to look after him. You must join the other women. Mawatani will join us when he returns."

The tokala, the group of men who served to keep order during travel, was there to make sure the move went smoothly. With a signal from them, the hunting party set out.

Each man took two horses; one to travel on and his best trained horse for transferring onto when the chase for buffalo began. Behind them, the women followed with pack horses to bring back the butchered meat.

The tiyospayes set up separate camps. Night Eagle's band settled on Rapid Creek. Bear Walker's group went further northwest, encamping on Spring Creek. Doing this, the men would be able approach the herd from above and below.

Seeing the smoke from the campfires ahead, Mawatani hurried Napasni to a gallop and was soon entering Night Eagle's camp. He stopped to speak with Night Eagle, who told him where his tiyospaye was encamped. Zicahota was out with the hunting party, so Mawatani continued to his own camp.

Just before reaching Spring Creek, he climbed a rise to spot their camp. There, almost due North, he spotted their fires.

Entering the camp, he saw that nearly everyone was out on the hunt. Only the very young and the old stayed at the site.

Some of the children came running toward him, excited to see him. One ran to the lodge of Talks With Owls to let him know Mawatani had returned. Chapa Winhaha ran through the crowd, his face beaming with a happy grin.

"Mawatani! Mawatani! You have come back."

"Of course I came back. I'm glad to see you too, misunkala. I am always glad to see my little brother."

Some older boys, including Six Toes and Catches Tail, were preparing to leave for the area where ptecincala, buffalo calves, had been chased by the men to an area away from the herd. This separation from the herd was done each hunt so the young boys could practice their hunting skills. Each boy was determined to catch a calf today.

"Mawatani," yelled Six Toes. "You are here in time to join us in the hunt."

"I'll join you later," Mawatani replied, "I must see Talks With Owls first. Go ahead, I will follow."

He approached Talks With Owls' lodge and announced himself.

"Enter," the old man replied.

Mawatani did not know how to begin. There was so much to say.

Talks With Owls sat facing the entrance, silent.

"I have done much thinking over the past few days," Mawatani began.

The old man said nothing.

"I have much to say," the boy continued. "I don't know where to start."

Still, Talks With Owls said nothing.

"I ask that you continue sharing your wisdom."

Talks With Owls stirred.

Mawatani was becoming self-conscious. *Is he angry with me? Disappointed? Why won't he answer?*

Finally, the old man motioned for him to sit.

"You did not tell me you were leaving," he said.

"Yes, I know; but everything was so confused in my mind. I couldn't think. I didn't know how to tell you I could not accept the honor of cutting the tree. All I could think of was getting away from all that was happening and sort out my thoughts."

"I understand that need," the old man said, "but no one knew where you were. We feared for you. We feared you were, once again, attempting to escape your problems."

"No!" Mawatani said emphatically. "Not escape them, grandfather, but become closer to them; study them; conquer them. I could not do that in the village. My thoughts were too confusing. I learned much while I was alone and wish to share all this with you."

"Then begin," Talks With Owls said.

"I will begin tomorrow," Mawatani said. "Today, I will join my friends in the hunt. This too, is important."

"Good," Talks With Owls agreed. "Hunt well, koskalaka, and respect tatanka. It is the sacred buffalo that gives us life."

"Yes, grandfather, I will." Mawatani started to leave, then turned back to the old man. "I should let my mother know I am here. Is she with the women on the hunt?"

"Yes. I have sent a young boy to tell her you have returned."

"Thank you, Grandfather. I will join my friends now."

As he rode out of the camp, the children yelled, "Wana seyaoi. They will chase the buffalo and catch a calf!"

As he reached the top of a rise, he could see his friends in the distance, chasing calves that seemed to be much smarter than they expected.

Suddenly, off to the south, he saw a lone cehinka tapte, a full-grown buffalo cow, running at full speed toward the area where his friends were. *She probably picked up the scent of her calf*. He put his legs into Napasni and rushed to warn the boys.

As he rode, he grabbed his bow. He could no longer see the cow because of the hill in front of him, but he was now near enough to warn his friends.

"Cehinka tapte! Cehinka tapte!," Mawatani yelled to his friends. "It is a large cow! Pte oweceya! Pte oweceya!! She is crying for her calf! Be ready!"

Mawatani turned toward where he thought the cow would be and pushed Napasni in that direction. Suddenly, the cow was almost on him. Quickly, he set an arrow to the bow and released it. It entered the right haunch of the animal but had very little effect.

He feared for Napasni, as he brought him alongside this huge beast. Many horses have been gored during the hunt, and Napasni was not trained for this. Without thinking, he jumped on the cow's back, but his timing was off. Mawatani landed on the hump and slid down to her neck. Grabbing on to the longer fur on her head, he struggled to stay on. Immediately, he realized this was not one of his better ideas. Being on a buffalo was nothing like being on a horse.

The cow began to toss her head to get him off. Mawatani wrapped his legs around her neck as he bounced around, barely able to hold on. His right leg could not bend enough to be effective and he began to slide off. Bending over her head, he caught her left horn. Pulling himself up, he grabbed the other horn and tried to turn her away from his friends.

The boys watched, trying to find a way to help. Catches Tail and Six Toes both had their arrows ready. They urged their horses to join the chase, bringing them as close to the cow as possible. These horses were also not trained to be around such a large creature and were skittish.

Six Toes was afraid he might hit Mawatani if he sent the arrow, but realized not shooting it might be worse. He released an arrow that entered the left side of the cow's ribs, causing it to veer directly towards Catches Tail.

Mawatani pulled at her horns with all his might in an attempt to change her direction. Catches Tail turned away and charged his horse alongside her, sending an arrow into one side of her neck, exiting the other side. Her windpipe was punctured, bringing her to her knees. Mawatani flew off. His head hit the ground with a thud and his body slid across the ground. His cousin came along side to pull him away.

Somehow, the cow regained her footing and began to chase again. Six Toes sent another arrow into the back of her neck and she fell. He ran to help Catches Tail, who was holding Mawatani off the ground as he rode.

Mawatani was dazed and wavered as he tried to stand. Blood ran from the scrapes he received and oozed from a lump that was already forming on his forehead. He was dizzy and breathless. After he caught his breath, a smile formed as he turned to the boys and began to laugh.

Mawatani raised his arms in triumph. "Oohiye! Oohiye! We have brought in a buffalo!" The others joined in and soon "Oohiye! Oohiye!" echoed through the prairie.

"Who needs calves?" Mawatani asked. "This year, we bring home a cow."

The boys began to whoop and dance, and their laughter filled the air. Mawatani was still dizzy and stumbling as he danced and laughed.

When their excitement diminished, the boys stopped and thanked the cow for her sacrifice so their people might live. They also apologized to the calf that now had no mother.

Remembering the problems they had butchering the elk just a short time before, they decided to send one of the boys back to camp to bring some of the older women to do the honors. It was late afternoon by the time the women had the meat ready to transport back to the village.

Mawatani was still excited about the adventure, but the reality of what he did was sinking in. The stupidity of it frightened him. He was amazed he wasn't killed. His body shook and he needed help to mount Napasni. He was already stiff and sore from the buffalo ride and the fall.

The boys would be honored tonight but would get none of the meat. That was how it was done when you made your first kill. This was to teach the young the kill was for the people, not for them. It would still be a glorious night of celebration.

By the time they neared camp, Mawatani was calm again; stiff, but calm.

The main hunting party had not yet returned when the boys rode into camp yelling and whooping. "We bring meat to the camp!"

The elderly and children went out to meet them. Seeing the bleeding wounds of Mawatani, the old women insisted that he go to the lodge of Cankuwasté to be treated for his cuts and bruises. The medicine man told him he was crazy to climb on the back of a grown buffalo. Then, he told him how brave he was to do it.

The boys were leaving the lodge when the men from the hunting party entered the village. The hunt was good, they were told. The women had more than enough to keep them busy. It would be a good winter for meat and hides.

To Mawatani, it seemed like forever before the women rode in. He saw his mother riding in front, eyes moving around the village, undoubtedly looking for him. When she saw him, her faced beamed and he casually nodded to her.

As Holy Moon Woman came closer and saw his injuries, she asked Six Toes what had happened.

"Nothing," Six Toes answered, "He just rode a buffalo cow that didn't want to be ridden."

Holy Moon Woman's eyes grew large, but Mawatani's grin told her that it was nothing serious.

That evening was one of much celebrating, and many prayers of thanks, for no creature on the earth were more sacred than the buffalo.

The aroma of roasting buffalo meat filled the air, and bellies were getting full. The boys made it through the evening eating everything but buffalo meat. They were proud of themselves and were honored to forgo the pleasure.

Dancing, singing and much talking went on far into the night. Mawatani decided to return to his lodge and sleep. His head was aching, and he was beginning to wonder if he would even be able to move next day. His body was already quite stiff from the fall. It didn't matter. He was happy. It had been a wonderful day.

The days following, were filled with preparing and drying the meat, and scraping hides. Some hides were soft tanned for parfleches, tipis, drums and clothing. Others were dried stiff for rattles and splints. Hooves were boiled for glue; horns, scraped thin for spoons and cups. Bones were scraped to hew into needles, awls and paint sticks. Stomachs and bladders were cleaned and dried to use as bags for food and water. Muscles and tendons were dried and split for thread, and sinew twisted for bow string. Many sets of ribs were given to the children to scrape clean to use as sleds during the winter.

During all of this, Mawatani spent much of his time with Talks With Owls. One of the first things he asked the old man was, "What happened to Matoska? He was not with us on the hunt."

"He told us he was sick," answered Talks With Owls. "I believe he did not feel ready to go with the men, and did not want to go with the hoksilas."

"What are we going to do about him?" Mawatani asked.

"Perhaps we will just have to wait to see if he wants to tell us what is wrong. It is a puzzle," Talks With Owls answered.

Mawatani began to tell him of all the thoughts that crowded his mind during his retreat near Cedar Butte.

The old man listened with wise ears and spoke of the never-ending circle of life. "The earth is round and the sky that enfolds it is round. The sun and the moon are round. The winds often whirl in circles. The seasons come and go, always in the same order to make a circle. All life is centered around a circle and when we see that, we are able to understand how we must lead our lives."

Mawatani felt more relaxed with the old man now than he did a few weeks ago; more prepared to take in his wisdom. There was something changed within his mind since his retreat. The thought of leaving the safety of his childhood was not as frightening as it was before. Part of the awe he felt for Talks With Owls turned to respect. Again, he thanked the Great Spirit for giving Him such a wise and holy teacher.

The time finally came to leave the temporary camp. Mawatani's tiyospaye had picked a new campsite on West Horse Creek. On the way, they would stop at the Battle Creek site where Night Eagle's people were. There, they would celebrate the successful hunt together and take time to visit and catch up on the news of relatives and friends. After a few days, they would head for their new camps.

Chapter 19

All Things Are Sacred

Since setting up their new camp, the business of preparation for winter made for long and busy days. The snow was already collecting on the north facing areas of the hills to the west and was falling in their area often. The cold was causing the creek to freeze in shallow areas.

With most of the work completed, a more relaxed atmosphere allowed groups of men to talk casually while the women met to sew and catch up on news. Children played and worked to get their buffalo rib sleds ready for the heavier snows to come.

Mawatani loved to watch Tahcawe play "Doing The Sliding." She was very good at throwing and hitting the other girl's 'smoke', the small red stick each girl had standing in front of her. She won almost every game, winning many necklaces and porcupine quills. She would seldom keep them, preferring to give a gift to the girls who lost. This way, each girl always had a stake to use at the game.

Mawatani's favorite winter game was "Throwing It In." It was played on ice with tops directed toward five holes. It was not easy to get them in the holes, but it was fun. The winner was the one who got his top in the middle hole. That was so hard to do, the game often had to be carried over to another day.

Mawatani often wondered how he let an entire year go by, not allowing himself to be a part of this wonderful life. His lame leg seemed insignificant compared to the life he had now. He wondered if his lameness was a message from Wakan Tanka. Perhaps this was the only way he would have learned the direction he was to follow; but at what cost? He was not thinking of the cost of the use of his leg, but of the loss of Steals Many Horses; that still hurt.

The days were becoming shorter and nights demanded heavier blankets. The green of the prairie was lost to hues of reds and yellows in the trees and bushes. Most of the grasses were an earthy brown. West Horse Creek flowed low and calmly, still providing the necessary water to the village, but reserving plenty of room for the moisture of winter.

During these days, Mawatani spent most of his time with Talks With Owls. The old man now emphasized the importance of wakan econpi, what we do; wakan iya, what we say; and wakan lowanpi, what we sing within our spiritual lives. "Always live your life to please the spirits. Spirits live in all things: the rocks, the grasses, and the trees; in drums, war clubs, and tipis; in the winged people, the four-leggeds and creatures of the waters.

"The good spirits will protect a good man from the mischief of the bad spirits. Burn sweetgrass and sage to honor them, for it is through them we learn what actions are best for us to take. We two-leggeds know only what has already happened. The spirits know all that, plus what is to take place. They are our guides to show us how we are to prepare.

"All we have talked about and all that we do is to honor Wakan Tanka. Our prayers and ceremonies help us to grow and flourish, like the rains of spring help the growing things on grandmother earth to blossom. They sustain us and prepare us to live in the real life when we leave this life."

Talks With Owls spoke of the importance of family, and how an individual had little power. A family group, joined by blood and support of each other, could have great power. A family of families, like a tiyospaye, could handle almost anything that confronted them.

"It is in the family that learning must take place. Without family, we are nothing. It is within the family we learn the value of hard work and to shun laziness."

What a remarkable and holy man he is, Mawatani thought. His respect for the old man was reverting to awe. *I will never reach the greatness and holiness of this man. They are beyond my reach; but that will be my goal.*

Over and over, Mawatani and Talks With Owls talked of the sacred hoop, and how everything in creation is part of the hoop. "Nothing exists outside of it. Everyone, everywhere, is a part of it. It is without time, always flowing. The circle is both symbol and reality. It is in the embrace of these two things that the harmony of life is expressed. We must continuously grow in the process of developing our spiritual self and gaining wisdom."

The old man told and retold many of the ancient Sioux legends. These are the stories that give flavor and meaning to their history.

The history of the Makosica was told through the tale of the Unktehi, the terrible water monsters. These serpents caused floods over all the land, killing many people. The Thunderbirds, who were compassionate, saw all this and began to wonder how they could help. The Thunderbirds waged many battles with the Untehi and showed the humans a high rock, where they told them to stay until the battle was won. Together, they released all their lightning bolts, setting the land on fire. Everything was consumed except for the rock where the people stayed. The waters boiled and dried up, leaving the earth glowing red hot. All the Untehi burned and died, leaving only their bones, which now make up the Makosica, the Badlands.

One lesson Mawatani was learning was one never discussed. He was beginning to understand the old man's long pauses during his time with him. The silent pauses were used to communicate with the spirits; to hear what they were telling him. Soon, he too, was using these silences to honor and acknowledge the spirits and listen to their messages. He was not very good at it yet, but he was learning.

Talks With Owls spent much of the time talking about the hanbleceya itself, immersing Mawatani in all the parts of the vision quest. There was much to learn as each ritual was solemn and had to be performed just as the spirits had taught them.

Sometimes, Mawatani's head would become so full of facts, he would take a break from his visits with Talk With Owls. Several times during the winter, when the weather was good, he would take Napasni and ride for a visit with Zicahota. On one such trip, his friend made an announcement:

"Bear Killer, I have something to tell you."

"So tell me, kola, what is it?" Mawatani asked.

"I too, am preparing for my hanbleceya. I thought I already knew the future for me with my people, but lately I have had other thoughts. I must learn what the spirits want me to do."

"What is this future you were so sure of?"

"Kola, I have always been a thunder dreamer. I had no doubt what the Spirits wanted of me. I was to be a heyoka, a contrary. I knew this since I was a small child. I was sure it would be my path.

"When I saw Hears The Voice and Walks In Silence do their medicine on your uncle, I began to wonder if I should wait until after my quest to see if my vision tells me something else. What they do is so good; so powerful. Something inside me is pointing me in this direction. Maybe I am to be some sort of medicine man, maybe something else. These thoughts are very new to me. I have spoken with Hears The Voice about it. He is helping my até to prepare me."

"I'm still not sure where my path leads," Mawatani said. "Talks With Owls says he sees my path clearly, but I must find it myself. You and I will help each other find our way."

The two placed an arm on each other's shoulders in friendship.

"Your quest will be first," Zicahota said, "and I will be there. At the next moon after yours, I will cry for a vision."

"And I will be there," Mawatani replied.

For many hours, they talked and wondered where their lives would take them.

PART V

HANBLECEYA

Chapter 20

The Time Is Here

Mawatani sat at the edge of West Horse Creek. With eyes closed, his mind reached out to mitakuye oyasin, all my relations, asking for their intercessions to the Great Spirit, to help him in his quest.

The waters of the creek were high with runoff from the winter snows. The sounds of the current told of the mysteries and sacredness of life; messages of Takuskanskan, the Spirit of all motion. This time and place were sacred.

He gazed westward toward the Paha Sapa that stretched to the Northwest as far as the eye could see. For centuries, the inhabitants of the area had climbed these hills in search of messages from the spirits. They symbolized all that was strong and solid. The people would forever thank Grandmother Earth for the gift of these sacred mountains.

As beautiful as the dawning of spring was, Mawatani was struggling to ward off the excitement and anticipation of the days ahead. This was the day he would make the ceremonial announcement of his hanbleceya. This morning, he would go to the lodge of Talks With Owls and formally declare that he was to begin his time of lamentation. He was ready for his vision quest.

Doubts and questions still stirred in his thoughts. *What if I'm not ready? What if the spirits are not ready to give me a vision? What if I fail in my quest?*

Yet, he knew Talks With Owls had prepared him well. *I have learned many remarkable things from this wise old man, he thought. I am ready.*

He stood, raised his arms to the heavens and cried, "Be with me, Wakan Tanka, as I cry for a vision."

With a deep sigh, he turned away from the creek and went to his lodge to get his pipe, a gift from Bear Walker. As he tied a bag of tobacco and kinnickinnick to his belt, Holy Moon Woman stood by the fire holding Comes Alone. Tahcawé and Chapa Winhaha sat on their mats, watching every move he made. They said nothing, for they knew this was a holy time for him.

Mawatani forced himself to walk slowly to meet with Talks With Owls. Stopping at the entrance of the old man's lodge, he calmed himself, slowing the pace of the drums that beat within his heart. He announced himself and entered, holding the stem of the pipe in front of him, and sat opposite the holy man. He turned the pipe stem to face himself, for he was the one who needed the blessings and knowledge for his quest.

Talks With Owls took the pipe and asked Mawatani for his kinnickinnick to fill it. After filling it, he raised it to the four directions, and then directed it to Grandfather and to Grandmother. He then asked, "What is your wish?"

"To seek a vision and offer my pipe to Wakan Tanka," Mawatani replied. "I ask for your guidance and intercession with the Great Powers."

"Hau. This is good," the old man answered.

Talks With Owls led Mawatani from the tipi and faced the West. Bear Walker, Catches Tail, Six Toes and Zicahota joined to make a circle.

As Talks With Owls raised his arms, those with him followed his lead. Four times they chanted, "Hey o." The old man then prayed:

"O Wakan Tanka, our Grandfather,
You are the one who has always been.
Never was there a time before you. Hear us.
We are sending our voices to you.
This young man will soon cry for a vision
and wishes to offer his pipe to you.
You, who guard our sacred pipe,
assist us and guide us.
We offer this pipe to you, Wakan Tanka,
asking for a blessing for this young man,
Mawatani."

Those standing in the circle cried out, "Hau," for this was a good prayer. They sat on the ground in a circle, with the exception of Talks With Owls, who offered the pipe again, then sat with the others. He lit the pipe, took three puffs, and offered it to Mawatani. When Mawatani was finished, it was passed around the circle. When it was empty, it was returned to the holy man. He filled it with tallow, as it could not be smoked during this first quest. The old man returned the pipe to Mawatani.

"This pipe is sacred, and you have come with it crying for a vision," Talks With Owls declared. "You must always remember what I have taught you and walk through life with all that you have learned. Now, when do you wish to begin this quest for a vision?"

"The morning after hanhepi wi has risen two more times," Mawatani replied.

"That is when it shall be," the old man responded. "How many days do you choose?"

"I choose four days."

This pleased Talks With Owls. Most young men chose two days.

"You have much to do to prepare for this sacred time, koskalaka," Talks With Owls said. "This is what must be done: first, you must build an inipi lodge where we will purify ourselves. To do this, you must find sixteen small willows. Remember what we learn from the willows. It is in the fall when they drop their leaves and appear to lose their lives; but in the spring they come to life again. The same is with us two-legged people. We live on this earth for a while and it seems we die, but we, too, live again, for it is only after we die that we really live. This is why we purify our bodies in the inipi; to become closer to Wakan Tanka.

"Remember, before cutting the willows, to take them an offering of tobacco. Let them know why you are taking them. You must tell them that, though there are many trees, it is the willow you have chosen to help you. Let them know that, even though they will no longer be here, others will take their place. After you have cut them, bring them back so the lodge can be built. All of this must be done in a sacred manner.

"You must also gather the rocks and sage to be used and make a bundle of five long sticks and twelve small sticks to use as offerings. These, you will lean against the west side of the initi, where they will stay until the time comes to purify them. You must also bring Ree Twist tobacco, kinnickinnick, a cutting board for the tobacco, and buckskin to use for the tobacco offerings. You will need sweetgrass, a pouch of sacred earth, a knife, and a stone hatchet. You must gather all these things yourself. Hecetu welo. This is the way it must be done."

Mawatani took his pipe and returned to his lodge.

Chapter 21

Anticipation

Mawatani learned all that he would need long before his announcement ceremony. Talks With Owls was more than thorough. The bundles for offerings were ready. The long and small sticks were gathered. He already chose the willow trees he would use for the initi. Taking his hatchet and a tobacco offering, he fastened a travois to Napasni and set off to cut the branches he would need. With the help of his three friends, they should be able to get a good start on the lodge today.

Mawatani asked Catches Tail and Six Toes to act as hosts to Zicahota while he was gone. The boys soon discovered that was not an easy task. Zicahota said little and seemed uncomfortable; as though he would rather be left alone.

"What is it Mawatani sees in him?" Catches Tail, whispered to Six Toes.

"I don't know," answered Six Toes. "He says practically nothing and will barely answer when spoken to."

After a fidgety time sitting and little else, Six Toes said, "Mawatani tells us that you handle a bow and arrow better than anyone in your tiyospaye. Show us."

Zicahota's eyes lit up with signs of interest. "Do you want to play 'See Who Shoots The Farthest'?" he asked.

"No," Catches Tail answered. "Let's just shoot at targets."

Zicahota ran to his horse and pulled out the bow of Mawatani's father. "Where shall we shoot?"

"There is a place by the creek," Six Toes said. "Let's go there."

When Mawatani returned with the willows that afternoon, the boys were still at the creek.

After unloading the trees and setting them at the site of the initi, he went to join them.

Zacahota stopped what he was doing and went to him. "Did you get all your trees?"

"Yes. We can begin to build the lodge now."

Catches Tail ran to him, shouting, "Mawatani, Zicahota has shown us ways to improve our shooting. Watch this," he said, placing an arrow in the notch.

"Not now, Catches Tail," Zicahota said. "Not now. This is a sacred time for Mawatani. We must help to keep it sacred. An arrow you can shoot any time. A koskalaka's first hanbleceya comes only once. Let us say a prayer that what we are about to do will be done in a sacred manner."

After Zicahota intoned a prayer, the boys went to build the inipi. They began to set up the poles, making sure the door would be to the east, for it is from the east that light comes, and light is wisdom. The three friends set the poles in place, carefully bending them from east to west and north to south. This was to symbolize the four directions. With each step of building, they said the necessary prayers.

As they did this, Mawatani stepped off ten paces from the entrance and marked the spot where he would build the peta owihankeshni, the fire of no end. This fire represented the power of Wakan Tanka, who gives life to all things. It is where the rocks would be heated. The rocks were used, not just to make the sacred steam, but they represented Grandmother, from whom all things of the earth come. The rocks also represented Wakan Tanka, for they are solid and everlasting like him.

Over the marked spot, Mawatani placed four sticks facing East and West. Over the sticks, he placed four sticks facing North and South. Other sticks, he leaned against these, as in making a tipi. He placed the rocks to be used at each of the four directions. As he did this, he prayed:

> "O grandfather, Wakan Tanka, I build this fireplace as we have been taught by you.
> I am preparing to humble myself in search of a vision so I may learn what you want of me in this life.
> As I place these stones at the four directions, my heart knows you are in the center, as you are the center of all things.
> My heart is full from this knowledge.
> Pilamaya. I thank you and rejoice, O sacred rocks, for you are helping me on my sacred journey."

As his friends finished placing the willows for the framework, Mawatani went to its center and began to build the central altar. He pushed a stick into the earth at the center of the space for the initi. Attaching a cord of rawhide to the stick, he drew a circle around it praying:

> "O Grandfather, creator of all that is, behold what I do here.

Grandmother Earth, whose holy ears
hear all that makes sound, hear me.
We come to this life with You and will
return to You when our spirit's journey
along the great path of this life ends.
By marking this center, I think of You,
O Wakan Tanka, the center of all things,
for our spirits will become as one.
I wish to become worthy of you so my
people may live."

Mawatani dug a round hole around the center stick. With the dirt from the hole, he made a path toward the East, that would lead to the peta owihankeshni, symbolizing the Sacred Path.

Time passed quickly; daylight turned to dusk. They would finish the lodge tomorrow.

Zicahota went to spend the night with Mawatani and his family.

During the evening meal, Mawatani began to notice Takcawe' placing much of her attention on Zicahota. At times, when she caught his eyes, she would lower her head shyly, and a girlish grin would appear.

This is not good, Mawatani thought, *yet, she is only nine summers old. I suppose it's nothing to worry about.*

Before retiring for the night, Mawatani left the lodge to spend some time alone. The night was cool and, off in the distance, lightning flashes illuminated the sky. So far this spring, the rains were moderate. Hopefully, that is the way it would remain. The floods of last year were not welcome.

The boys headed out early the next morning. When they reached the site of the initi, they found a good part of their work from yesterday had been destroyed. Willow branches from the framework were strewn about the area. The path Mawatani had so carefully crafted was in disarray.

Mawatani stared in disbelief.

As anger grew within him, Catches Tail shouted, "This has to be the work of Etonka!" As he turned toward Etonka's lodge, he said, "I'm going to show him the color of his blood."

"No!" Mawatani grabbed him by the arm. "We must not let him ruin this holy time by our bad behavior. We will begin again and stay focused on what we are doing. When I return from the mountain we will deal with Etonka."

Six Toes ran to Mawatani. "But Mawatani, he will think he got away with it!"

"What he thinks at this moment is not important," Mawatani replied. "The only things of importance at this time are the initi and our remaining true to our task. Anger must be set aside to do that. We will say a prayer to help us do this."

After the prayer, the boys began their work.

Behind a tree nearby, Etonka wore a smile of satisfaction.

The boys worked at a feverish pace, yet remained focused on the holiness of their task.

Mawatani began working on the dirt path. As he placed the loose dirt on its eastern course, he prayed:

> "O Grandmother Earth, upon You I build this sacred path of life.
> By purifying ourselves in the inipi we shall walk this path with sure and confident steps, for this path leads to Wakan Tanka.

May our people always walk this path in purity so we may live again in the real World."

At the end of the path, Mawatani built a small mound. It was on this mound that Talks With Owls' sacred pipe would rest. His own pipe, filled with tallow until after his hanbleceya, would rest next to it.

By early afternoon, the hides had been placed over the framework and the initi was completed.

The day turned very warm for spring. The boys went to the creek to wash and cool off. After thanking Catches Tail and Six Toes, Mawatani and Zicahota went to see Talks With Owls to see if he had any final instructions.

After their evening meal, Mawatani and Zicahota returned to the creek, listening to the music of the water. There was little said; an occasional comment about the sound of a bird or the gurgling of water, as it entered a jumble of roots, exposed after last year's floods.

Soon after the sun set, Zicahota broke the silence.

"Kola, you should go to your lodge and begin your sleep now. You will need it for the days ahead, when there will be little sleep."

"Yes, I know," Mawatani answered. "I don't think sleep will come easily tonight. My mind and heart are so full, but you're right. Come, let us return to the lodge."

"You go ahead," Zicahota replied. "I will stay here tonight and pray for the success of your hanbleceya."

"You will do that for me?" Mawatani asked.

"Of course." Then, with a smile, Zicahota added, "I will also make sure you are up early tomorrow. We wouldn't want to sleep in on such an important day."

After placing his arm on Zicahota's shoulder, Mawatani headed for his lodge. *How good it is to have this friendship,* he thought. *It strengthens me for what I am about to do.*

Chapter 22

The Quest

<u>Day 1</u>

During the inipi, Catches Tail and Six Toes brought three horses to the initi, including Napasni. Two carried the offering sticks, the poles, a bag of kinnickinnick, sage and all that would be needed at the site of the hanbleceya. Leaving Napasni, they went up to the site of the crying for a vision. There, they were to prepare the area as Talks With Owls taught them.

They put all the equipment in the center and dug a hole where they placed some kinnickinnick. After tying some of the offerings to a long pole, they placed it in the hole facing the East. Catches Tail took another pole with offerings, walking ten strides to the West, and set it up there. He did the same at the other two directions, returning to the center each time.

During this time, Six Toes made a bed of sage at the center, so when Mawatani became tired, he could rest his head against the center pole with his feet facing the East. Using the soil that came from the holes he dug, he built a mound to support Mawatani's pipe.

The inipi had been long. Mawatani was first to leave the lodge, praying humbly, as he walked the sacred path he had laid, and sat upon it. He faced the small mound built as a resting place for the sacred pipe.

Zicahota came to him with a buffalo robe that had been purified and placed it over Mawatani's shoulders. Bear Walker raised Mawatani's pipe up from the mound and reverently placed it in the boy's hands. His nephew was now ready to go to the mountain.

Mawatani mounted Napasni, holding the pipe in front of him. Talks With Owls, Bear Walker, and Zicahota joined him, heading for the mountain.

By the time they reached the waiting place at the foot of the mountain, the two boys had completed their work, and went to meet Mawatani.

Mawatani began his climb to the place that would be his alone for the next four days. All but Zicahota returned to the village. He wanted to stay nearby for a while. The next moon would be here soon. It would then be him that sought a vision. He wanted to think about this for a while.

Reaching the area his friends had prepared, Mawatani laid his pipe against the mound. He took off his robe and laid it on the ground. Earlier, he decided that he would not cover himself unless he became so cold it hampered his ability to stay centered. Taking off his moccasins, wearing only a breechcloth, he raised his arms to the skies, crying:

"Wakan Tanka, onsimala yo oyate nipikte wacin ca!" which means, O Great Spirit, be merciful to me, that my people may live.

Walking directly to the center pole, he stood, facing the East. Raising his pipe, he repeated the prayer: "Wakan Tanka onsimala yo oyate nipikte wacin ca!"

Excitement coursed through his body, but he remembered what Talks with Owls had taught him.

I must remember not to hurry my prayers. I must remain centered on what I am doing and never lose sight of the sacredness of this time.

Mawatani walked to the pole standing to the West. Crying the same prayer, he returned to the center pole. He repeated this ritual at the poles to the North and South, each time, returning to the center. After he made the prayer to the four directions, he raised his pipe to the sky asking for the help of Grandfather and all the winged people. Pointing it to the earth, he asked all that grew and rested on Grandmother Earth be with him and assist him during his time.

The first few hours went quickly as he stood in solitude, repeating the ceremony between the poles. Talks With Owls coached him well in the techniques of keeping his mind clear and open to accept any messages from the Great Spirit. His self-confidence soared and he knew that his quest would be successful.

As the day progressed, Mawatani thought of the time spent in his private retreat near Cedar Butte. He felt the same freedom now and treasured it. He remembered mounting Napasni and galloping through the brush and grasses of the prairie with the wind in his face. Oh, the exhilaration, the pure joy of that feeling!

With a start, he realized his mind had wandered from its centeredness. He was no longer focused on his quest. The thoughts in his head became noisy, making it impossible to hear any message that Wakan Tanka might be sending.

His body felt tired as he noticed the sun, now far to the west. He had been standing for a long time. Apologizing to Wakan Tanka for having such a weak spirit, he lay with his head to the center pole and his feet to the East.

I will not lie here long, he told himself, *and I will not allow myself to go to sleep. My body just needs a short time to rest.*

The thoughts running through his mind now were a jumble, and he knew he must quiet them before he could ever hope to receive a vision. Once again, returning to the discipline taught by Talks With Owls, he began to methodically extract one unruly thought at a time. If he had not learned one other thing from the holy man, this exercise was worth all the time. It was almost like a game.

As his mind grew quieter, it became difficult not to give in to sleep, but he was determined not to let that happen. *This is only the first day.* He had pledged not to let himself sleep for at least two days. Maybe after that he would have to listen to his body's need for rest; but not yet.

As darkness pushed the remnants of sunlight down the far side of the Paha Sapa, his body became more relaxed. Only the ache in his right leg kept him from separating his mind from his body. He would have to push the pain aside. His open mind must become the center of his being, otherwise, he would not be open to receive the vision he so desperately wanted. The vision was more important than the pain.

It took more time than he hoped, but he was again centered and open to receive a message from the spirit world. His pain did not leave him, but was now a part of his being, a sensation, but not a distraction. He became one with his surroundings.

By regaining control of his thoughts, he no longer had to fight off sleep. He was completely relaxed, hearing the night sounds of the prairie; the howl of a coyote; the hoot of an owl, and the conversations of other winged people of the night. He lost track of time. Soon he would get up and begin the ritual of prayers at the poles again.

Day 2

The night was cold, and the early morning turned even colder when the sun first rose over the horizon. Mawatani shivered and almost reached for his robe but stopped himself. *I have spent only one night. I cannot give in to the weakness of my body so soon. I have only to wait. The air will become warmer as anpetu wi moves higher in the sky.*

He was right. A short time ago, the little bumps on his skin that come with the cold, had covered his body. He always thought those bumps made him look like a winged person that had just been plucked. Now that the air was being warmed by the sun, the bumps were disappearing. His leg still ached and was stiff and weak from the effects of the cold, but he was ready to take on the new day. *Today will be the day I receive my vision,* he thought. *This will be a good day.*

The sun continued its journey across the sky as Mawatani continued his prayers. He repeated the circular passage from the center pole to those at the four directions. He thanked the spirits for his good life and for the love that Tunkasila showed his people. At the end of each circuit, he would take the pipe and offer it up. He would then stand, with arms outstretched to the sky, begging for a vision.

As the sun reached the top of the sky and continued to the West, Mawatani began to find it more difficult to remain centered. Thoughts, outside his quest, began to creep into his prayers. Even his body began to speak, as his stomach rolled from hunger.

This isn't working, he thought. *I must be doing something wrong.*

As these thoughts ran through his mind, he heard the voice of Talks With Owls in his head. "You must have patience and perseverance to be successful in your quest." *Patience. Talks With Owl used that word over and over. I am not good at patience. I must find my center again and not think of my tiredness or my hunger, only of my quest for a vision. That is all that is important.*

Again, he began the task of emptying his mind of everything that was not connected to his quest. He was becoming quite good at it now. By late afternoon he was doing well in keeping out the thoughts of hunger and frustration. His fasting and prayer led him, again, into that near trance he achieved earlier. His mind was again free from anything but openness to a message from some spirit who had an interest in his life journey.

The hours passed quickly, as he stood waiting for a messenger from Wakan Tanka. Hanhepi wi neared the center of the sky before he allowed himself to sit and rest his body.

After a short rest, he stood again, returning to walking the pattern of the poles. His mind was prepared to hear a message.

Day 3

The night went well. Before Mawatani even realized it, day three was already well underway. The sun passed the center of the sky some time ago, but so far this new day brought nothing in the way of a vision. He had still not slept, forcing his body to remain alert and his mind open to the spirits. Throughout the night, he repeated the ritual of the poles many times. He felt he was successful in doing these rituals. Still, there was no message; no vision.

I wonder if Talks With Owls would still be patient. How much patience can one have?

His frustration was beginning to take its toll. *Why is nothing happening? I have done all I was instructed to do. I have performed all the rituals over and over, and have prayed as I have never prayed before. O Wakan Tanka, what else is it you want of me? I have remained standing in your presence most of my time here, lamenting and humbling myself, but nothing has happened. Is my lamenting lacking? Is my humility not enough? Almost three days have passed, and still you have not sent a vision.*

During the day he continued praying, asking the spirits of the four directions and mitakuye oyasin to intercede for him.

Remaining centered was now becoming more difficult. He was near, but not quite entered into, a state of trance. He was no longer able to keep his thoughts separated. They were muddled and unorganized, impossible to follow.

My fasting and keeping myself from sleeping should have pleased the spirits. What am I doing wrong? There must be something I can do to please them. I am so tired, and my leg aches so bad I can barely stand it. My thoughts are like grains of sand slipping through my mind. I have to lie down and rest. I'll try to stay awake, but if I sleep, I sleep.

The sun was now far to the West and falling behind the Paha Sapa, leaving a dramatic silhouette of the many peaks that made up the holy mountains.

So far, he managed not to sleep and was close to being centered again. Feeling much more relaxed now, he lay in a relatively quiet calm.

Soon, he reached the point where time meant nothing: a true trance. Barely aware that he was separate from the world around him, his body felt adrift, floating freely among the star spirits. He remained in this state until, in the quiet, he heard a rustling in a nearby bush and the sound of a whimper.

He focused on the sound. It grew closer, so he got up and looked around. In the darkness, beyond the South pole, he saw two eyes looking up at him. At first, he was frightened, but soon realized it was a young wolf. Looking closer, he noticed it was injured; its right rear leg dangled loosely. For some reason, Mawatani was not afraid of this wild animal. He knew he was not supposed to leave the confines of his area of lamentation, but he could not just ignore this injured four-legged.

He walked toward the pup and held out his hand. The wolf came closer, smelled his hand, and nuzzled it.

"What happened to you, little kola?" The creature remained calm. Mawatani sat with him and examined his leg as best he could in the moonlight. He discovered the leg was not only broken, it was connected to his body only by skin. *Another four-legged must have attacked him,* he thought.

Mawatani went back to the poles to get his knife, and returned to the pup. "There is no way we can save your leg, little kola. You must be brave as I do this." The young wolf had to be in horrific pain but remained amazingly calm. It didn't even flinch as Mawatani took his knife and cut the bloody skin, severing the useless leg. Taking a piece of his breechcloth, he bound the stump.

This is a strange wolf to allow me to do this, he thought. *For some reason, I don't fear him.* After a pat on the head, the injured creature lay down where he stood and went to sleep.

It did not take long for Mawatani to return to that state of openness required to receive a vision. In fact, tending the wolf seemed to calm him, though he was unable to reenter the state of floating with the spirits. He repeated the ritual of the poles, pleading "Wakan Tanka onsimala yo oyate nipikte wacin." He was very confident again. He was sure that his quest would be successful.

Day 4

Much to Mawatani's displeasure, his calm began to dissolve, and his mind refused to cooperate with his needs. *Why is this? I have tried so hard. What is it that keeps my mind so cluttered and unable to remain open to a vision? Perhaps the spirits don't consider me worthy. If they don't, how can I convince them that I am?*

In attempting to figure out a reason for his failure, he decided it was the interruption by the wolf that caused this latest problem. *How can I remain focused on my quest when the spirits send an injured four-legged to interrupt my prayers and meditation? My time is almost up. My hanbleceya is a failure. I will have to return home and spend more time in preparation.*

In terrible disappointment, he asked Wakan Tanka to forgive him for his insufficient study, preparation and humility. *I am embarrassed that I took your gift of a vision for granted. I will do better next time.*

Preparing to leave, Mawatani picked up his robe and his pipe. After walking a few steps, he stopped. *Wait. I can't give up so easily. I still have time. I will try once more.*

He limped over to the center pole, raised his tired arms to Grandfather. He began, again, to put all thoughts out of his mind.

Eventually, his mind calmed and he felt prepared to receive a message. No longer were his thoughts on sleep or food or frustration. *Maybe there is still a chance the spirits will speak to me. I have confidence that I am prepared for a vision.*

He returned to prayer and lost track of time. His concentration broke when he heard a rustling in the brush ahead. He assumed the wolf had returned and, at first, ignored it. When the rustling continued, he looked toward the sound, but did not see the four-legged. Following the sound, it led him to a young eagle, with a broken wing.

"What happened to you, blessed eagle? Such a young and holy winged person should not have a broken wing. Let me see if I can help you."

Snapping off a straight limb from a tree, he bound the wing, using the rest of his breechcloth. *Now I have truly humbled myself. I am naked before the spirits and the world.*

He carefully laid the bird next to the bush where he found him.

Grandfather, why do you insist on sending me these interruptions? Each day I have stood waiting for a vision. Each day I have chanted the prayers, telling of my unworthiness. I have cried for a vision. Instead of granting me this, you have sent a wolf for me to tend; a wolf who is now as lame as I am. Then you sent an injured eagle that can no longer fly.

My arms ache from holding them up to you. My leg aches more than I can even explain. My body is cold. Even my breechcloth has been used to mend the wounds of the four-legged and the winged person. I am spent. Now I have truly failed.

In complete exhaustion, he lay down and fell into a deep sleep. The night was still dark when a cold, wet nose woke him with a start. In the moonlight, he saw the three-legged wolf standing next to him, nudging his face. A few feet away, the eagle was perched on the center pole with wings outstretched. There were no bandages on either of them. The wolf rose and went to the foot of the center pole. Both he and the eagle stared at Mawatani with unblinking eyes. Finally, the eagle blinked, and his resonant cry filled the air. The wolf and the eagle look toward each other. The wolf then looked up toward Grandfather and his howl echoed across the plains.

As Mawatani watched this, time seemed to stop for the moment. The silence of the prairie was suddenly filled by the resounding hoot of an owl. Mawatani watched in awe as the eagle took flight and circled above as the three-legged wolf raced toward the South. The cry of the owl filled the air again. The wolf halted his run and emitted a plaintive howl. These voices were sent as a message to Wakan Tanka. The wolf continued his run to the South until he disappeared in the distance. The eagle winged its way East until it became a spot in the distance, then vanished. There was complete silence.

Mawatani stood in this eerie silence trying to comprehend what just took place. He raised his arms to the skies. "Great Spirit ... Grandfather, how did this happen? What happened to their bindings? How did they heal so quickly? Please keep these two creatures safe in your care for they have been through much hardship."

As he attempted to fathom all this, the failure of his hanbleceya began to crowd his thoughts. He pleaded with Wakan Tanka for insights into plans for a lame boy who is not even able to receive a vision.

Though he remained standing, with arms raised, for what seemed to be hours, he received no reply from the spirits.

Day 5

A clap of thunder woke Mawatani to a new reality. He was lying in the middle of a cloud-burst, with his head at the center pole. He was soaking wet.

It is strange to have the Thunderbeings when the sun is just beginning to rise, he thought. Standing, he was at the end of his time of his first hanbleceya, and he had failed.

I have received no vision. I don't understand. I tried so hard, and thought I did all I could to prepare. Talks With Owls was a wonderful teacher. He will be disappointed by my failure.

Wakan Tanka, I am so confused. It took me three days to have a vision where very little happened. I didn't even prepare for that. The spirits sent me that vision and I didn't even ask for it. Now, I have spent four days crying for a vision and you have sent me a four-legged and a winged person to mend. I do not understand your ways. Tunkashila, help me.

He stood, dejected, and more tired than he had ever felt in his life. *I will lament no longer. I will no longer cry or beg for a vision. I have done all I can do. I am leaving this place.*

Though the rain was almost stopped now, his body shivered, and he became aware of the cold. He reached for his robe and, as he went to put it on, he made a startling discovery: he saw his breechcloth was whole.

He dropped his robe. *How is this possible? I used my breechcloth to mend the wolf and the eagle. How am I now wearing it? What has happened?*

Grandfather, I'm frightened. I don't understand this. Are you sending me a message? If so, I don't hear it.

He could not remember any time in his life when he had been so confused. He was so tired it was hard to concentrate. His body was too tired to remain standing, so he sat at the foot of the center pole.

I must try to sort this out. Why would the spirits give me a breechcloth? What kind of message is that? I have humbled myself by being here naked before them. Did I not even do that right?

Wanting to study each event as it took place, he began to look back on his time here, but being so exhausted, it was difficult.

The sun's warmth began to dry the land by late morning. As he sat in confusion, a thought suddenly came to him.

Wait! Let me think about this. He quickly rose and went to the bush where he found the wolf. There was no blood there. *The wolf lost much blood here. Where is it now?*

The reality hit him. *Can this be true? I don't believe it. It was so real, it must have happened... but, it couldn't have.*

Grandfather... was there no wolf, no eagle? What I remember in my mind never really happened? Then you did send a vision; a great vision; but what does it mean?

He went over the last few hours; or was it the last few days? *If this really was a vision, how long did it take? What day is this? How much of what I think took place really happened? What was real? What part was the vision? If this really was a vision, what message did it bring?*

Excitement began to build within him. *I think...I think I had a vision; an incredible vision.*

This required a different kind of thinking now. He must look at what happened in a different light. What did he really see?

I know Talks With Owls and the others will help me to interpret all this, but I need to understand some of it now.

Mawatani began to pray to the four directions, going from each pole to the center. He asked the spirits that dwelt there to please help him understand the message he had received. When he completed the circuit, he sat at the center, facing the east, studying each memory of his time there. Time was lost to him now. He had no idea how long he had been there. *Did I really stand for what seems like days praying for this vision, or was that part of the vision?*

Perhaps if I concentrate only on the two creatures that came to me, I will begin to understand. You showed me a lame wolf and a lame eagle, but what does it mean?

It was difficult to make sense out of any of this. Finally, a possibility came to him. *They were both lame but were living their lives as they were born to do. Their limitations did not hinder them. Perhaps it is as simple as that. Why weren't they sent as lame, and not injured? Was that so I would attempt to heal them; at least treat them? But they were not real, they were only spirits. Does Wakan Tanka want me to try to heal the spirits of my people? What do the cries of the owl mean?*

As these thoughts whirled through his mind, he made a decision. *This is too much for me to ponder on my own. I'll return to the tiyospe. After the inipi, I will ask for the assistance of those wiser than I am,*

He raised his arms to the sky thanking the spirits who had sent him this powerful message.

"Grandfather, forgive my doubts. You have given me a wonderful message. I will take it to Talks With Owls and the elders. They will help me interpret its full meaning. I will listen to their counsel and follow it.

"I am beginning to see my path, and it is a difficult one. If this is the path you want me to take, I will work hard and become the wisest and best wicasa wakan I can be. Talks With Owls has been a wonderful example for me. If I could be half as wise as he is, I too, could help my people. You have shown me my future. Now I must learn exactly what that future is and how to prepare for it." His tired body and mind felt suddenly renewed and the spirit within him soared as the eagle had soared.

He left his robe, where it would stay for four days, and took leave of the holy place of his vision. After a short distance, Bear Walker, Talks With Owls and Zicahota joined him. They waited some time, for this was the late morning of the fifth day. The ride to the village was in silence.

As they walked, the others sensed that Mawatani was very waken, very holy. It was obvious he had received a vision. Zicahota was thrilled for his friend. He couldn't help but think of his own quest at the next moon.

Mawatani's mind continued to pray in thanksgiving, pleading for the strength of character he would need to continue on this path he had been shown. As excited as he was about his vision, he was also frightened by its prospects.

He was anxious to tell his story to Talks With Owls, but his body and his mind were beginning to shut down. It became obvious the inipi would have to wait until tomorrow. Right now, he barely knew who he was.

They arrived at Mawatani's lodge where his mother had food waiting for him. He did not even stop to acknowledge it. He stumbled to his bed mat and was asleep immediately.

Seeing disappointment in the face of Holy Moon Woman, Bear Walker said "Take Heart, Holy Moon Woman. His need for sleep is greater than his need for food now."

"That is true," replied Talks With Owls. "Let him sleep until he wakes, then, he will eat. After that, we will meet in the initi to pray for understanding. He will be weak for a few days, but that will pass."

Chapter 23

· · · · · · · · · · · · · · ·

The End of The Beginning—
The Dawn of Tomorrow

Most morning chores were finished when Mawatani awoke. As he tried to stand, everything seemed to swirl and sway; the lodge appeared to be filled with a heavy fog. He fell back on his mat.

"It is no surprise that you stumble," his mother said, "Your body is starved. You must eat, Mawatani. Talks With Owls made me promise to make you eat before you meet the men at the initi."

Mawatani was not about to argue the point. He was famished and groggy. It was now more than five days since he had eaten. Carefully and slowly, he stood and walked to his meal. He was told many times by Talks With Owls that, when you fast for a long time, you must eat only small portions; slowly at first, and drink much water. He was still hungry when he finished but took the old man's advice to heart.

He was nearing the waiting men when he saw Etonka hiding behind his lodge, staring at him. *I must talk with him,* Mawatani thought, *and soon.*

What Mawatani did not know is, Talks With Owls had called Matoska to his lodge during his quest. The old man had not minced his words in chastising the boy for his behavior.

When Mawatani reached the initi, Talks With Owls asked if he was rested and if he had eaten. Mawatani assured him he had done both. The men entered to begin the ceremony.

Talks with Owls chose Bear Walker and another elder to aid in interpreting Mawatani's vision after the inipi.

This ceremony was much the same as the last. Many of the prayers were even the same, but the longer it lasted, the more Mawatani realized how different it was for him; far beyond anything he could express. Feelings swept through him; new feelings, unlike any he had ever experienced. Some of these feelings were probably enhanced by his weakness and, he was still on an emotional high from his quest. The prayers were more powerful, more meaningful. Their words had a life of their own.

The combined aromas of the sage, sweetgrass and kinnickinnick added to the dreamy state he was in. The holiness of what they were doing was so real, as if it was a living thing. This was wonderful! Incredible! The prayers and chants, the smells and the intense feeling of the sacredness of the moment, left Mawatani in a state of awe. He was not even aware when the ceremony ended. Only when the men stood did he realized it was over. He didn't want it to be over. He wanted it to go on forever.

"Come now, Mawatani," Talks with Owls said. "We will go to my lodge and learn of your vision."

Bear Walker gave Mawatani a hand up and they walked toward the old man's lodge. On the way, Mawatani saw Etonka again, but did not allow his mind to wander into everyday life. He wanted to keep the feeling within him as long as possible.

The men sat, each facing one of the four directions. The pipe was filled and lit. The offerings were made, and the proper prayers were intoned. When the pipe ceremony was completed, Talks With Owls sang a prayer, asking for the knowledge to interpret the story they were about to hear.

Mawatani hesitated. He was so filled with emotion he was having trouble speaking. After a long pause, he asked, "Where do you want me to start?"

"The beginning is usually a good place," answered Talk With Owls.

"But nothing happened at the beginning," Mawatani answered.

"Ah," the old man said. "I have never heard of a time when nothing happened. How do you explain this time of nothing?"

"I mean, I had no vision at the beginning. I did all the things you taught me. In fact, I did them many times, and in a sacred way. For three days I did these things. I am not sure when the vision began because I did not know I was having a vision. Even when I began to leave on the fourth day, I was unaware that I had received a vision. I thought I had failed. Then I sensed that something was not right, or as I thought. It was then I realized I succeeded. I remained another day to try to sort things out."

"This is what we wish to hear," the old man said.

"It was during the night of the third day," Mawatani began, "at least, I think it was the third day that it began. I was resting when I heard a sound in the bushes nearby."

He continued his story of the injured wolf and the eagle with a broken wing. It was told in such a manner that each man could see what the boy saw... could feel the warmth and caring of each act of kindness he performed on these creatures.

He told them of his nakedness, and of his amazement at seeing the wolf run and the eagle fly after caring for them. He spoke of the penetrating, echoing hoot of the owl, and the deafening howl of the wolf. He explained it was not until he noticed his breechcloth, that he realized he had a vision.

The men were impressed with the vision and the boy's telling of it. It was then, they began to search for the meaning.

Much time passed, as the men talked. Bear Walker wondered if it meant he was to become a healer of some kind. Talks With Owls thought about this and, to his way of thinking, that was not the message. The other elder wondered if the morning thunder held a message. After speaking of all these things, they came to the conclusion that Mawatani's interpretation was probably the most accurate. Mawatani was sure the true meaning would be clear after much meditation.

"You still have much to learn," Talks With Owls said, "but you have great wisdom for a koskalaka. I believe this learning should come from me. It is why you heard the cry of an owl."

Talks With Owls mentioned some of Mawatani's gifts and traits. "You show great compassion for all the earth people and all of Grandmother's gifts. This is an important thing. You think well and understand the circle of life and the medicine wheel. You have humility. Some think humility is a weakness. I believe it is a strength, as long as it comes from self-confidence. You will become a fine wicasa wakan. Many people will find comfort in your wisdom.

"It will take much time to understand all the vision has told you. You might still be finding new understandings when you are a grown man. Visions continue to define our lives as we grow older. Further quests will give you more insight."

After passing the pipe again, the men asked Mawatani if he was going to take a new name to symbolize his vision. Mawatani said he had not thought about it yet. Many possible names were offered. It was up to the boy to choose a name if he wished. He would consider the names carefully. If he decided to take a new name, he would probably carry it for the rest of his life.

The meeting was over. Mawatani's head was spinning, partly because he was still tired and hungry, but mainly from hearing his future set before him. It was a lot to take in. As he walked toward his lodge, he saw Etonka up ahead.

"Matoska," he called. "Come, let us talk."

Matoska paused, then walked up to Mawatani. He seemed subdued and nervous.

"Tell me, kola," Mawatani began, "what are we going to do about our friendship? You do not seem to like me anymore. What have I done to offend you?"

Matoska looked at him meekly. "I have been a fool, Mawatani. Talks With Owls took me into his lodge while you were gone. He made me see how wrong and dishonorable I have been. Mawatani, I became frightened when you took over the leadership of the hoksilas. I didn't know what to do. I was afraid to join the older boys. They are too much for me. I have tried to join in with them, but it just doesn't work. They can do things I am not able to do; some things I'm not even interested in doing. I don't belong with them. I can't find a place to belong. What do you do when you don't belong anywhere?"

Mawatani was amazed at what he was hearing. *No wonder he has been acting like this,* he thought. *He's scared. I guess I would be too.*

Matoska continued. "Talks With Owls told me that when you started to grow up you matured just as you should have, but you were maturing faster than the other boys; even faster than me. In my heart, I understood everything he said about my behavior, but I still clung to the jealousy and fear. I was even jealous of your bravery when you saved Bear Walker. It was when you returned from your quest that I realized what a fool I have been. Mawatani, you are who I want to be, but it is not in me. I never meant the things I said. I'm so sorry,"

"You are forgiven, Matoska."

"When my father was preparing me for my first quest I, too, spent time with Talks With Owls," Matoska continued, "I tried to learn the stories, and prepare for my hanbleceya, but my mind got all mixed up with the things he tried to teach me. That's why I'm not successful when I cry for a vision. I don't understand what I am supposed to be doing. I don't understand anything."

Mawatani put his hand on Matoska's shoulder and said, "Let us go sit in back of your lodge for a few minutes, kola." Matoska was near tears, as they sat.

"Matoska, do you know the large horse that belongs to Six Toes's father... the white one?"

"Yes," Matoska answered.

"Have you seen him run?"

"Yes, he is slow and can't keep up."

"That's right," Mawatani replied. "He is a good and sturdy horse, but slow. Does that make him less of a horse?"

"I guess not, but he does not have the value of a swift horse."

"He has great value when pulling a travois. He can out pull any horse in the village."

"What does this have to do with me?" Matoska asked.

"We all have value, Matoska. Sometimes we have to work hard to find what it is, where we fit. Do you know what we can do?"

"What?"

"During the next moon I will be with Zicahota preparing for his hanbleceya. I promised to be one of his helpers. When that is done, you and I will spend time together. I will help you to prepare. I do not have the wisdom of Talks With Owls, but I believe I can help. You will learn what you need."

"You would do that for me, after the way I treated you?"

"That time is past, Matoska. We will work together, and you will discover that you can be much more than you believe you can. You must begin to learn who you are. Do you remember when you learned about the medicine wheel when you were a small boy? I know that it is hard to understand its true meaning when you are young, but you must continue to learn. You must understand the meaning it holds in every day of your life and learn to live by what it teaches."

Matoska looked to the ground. "I remember my father trying to make me understand, but I couldn't keep up with what he said. It is too complicated."

"It doesn't have to be, Matoska," replied Mawatani. "What the medicine wheel tells us is, we must learn to know all sides of ourselves before we can become a whole person. From the West, we learn to look within ourselves to discover who we are. If we don't know who we are we are unable to know others. We must look to the North to gain in wisdom. If we do not have wisdom we are unable to interpret what is best for our people. From the East we will learn to be open to the possibilities that exist for us. The South is where we learn to always keep the innocence of our youth alive and retain trust. Without knowing all four sides of ourselves we are incomplete; not a whole person. Knowing ourselves brings the peace and tranquility that is our goal in life.

"While I am with Zicahota, spend time thinking of these things. Only then, can you prepare for your hanbleceya."

As Mawatani was walking away, he turned back to Matoska. "I will see that you are no longer called Etonka. I promise you."

"Thank you, kola," Matoska answered, "I am glad I can call you friend again."

"Now I have two things to celebrate," Mawatani said. "I have my friend back."

As Mawatani walked toward his lodge, Matoska called to him. "I'm happy for you, Mawatani." He continued to watch until Mawatani entered his lodge.

Mawatani decided to go to the creek, to sit and be alone. He must study the names that had been suggested and some of his own ideas. There were several. He did not have to change his name. Many young men wanted to take on a new name after they received a vision. Some names, he liked better than others, but they were all good names.

He tried out each name and imagined himself being called by it. Some didn't work at all. A few had possibilities. He went through this naming process for quite some time. After much study, he made his decision and went back to his home.

On his way, he ran into Zicahota, who was leaving Bear Walker's lodge.

"Bear Walker told me about the meeting, but not about your vision," Zicahota said. "He said that was for you to do, if you wanted."

169

"Of course I want to tell you." Mawatani looked to the sky to see where the sun was. "We have time now." They returned to the creek.

Zicahota listened intently to the story of the wolf, the eagle, and the hoot of the owl. When the story was over, they talked about what had been discussed at the meeting. Zicahota added some of his thoughts. He then asked Mawatani if he was going to take a new name.

"You will learn that with the others," Mawatani replied.

As evening came, the people began to gather for an informal get-together, where they could hear about Mawatani's vision. Though the night was cool, the people were warmed by this relaxing time with friends and family.

As evening turned into night, Talks With Owls quieted the people. It was time for Mawatani to tell his story.

Mawatani stood, looking at the crowd. *These are my people. Grandfather, help me to help my people.*

He told the story of his vision slowly, with great feeling and reverence. He explained how it had been interpreted and what it might mean for his life.

"I am sure my vision contains many more messages that have yet to be revealed. Of one thing I am sure; my life will be dedicated to you. All I do will be for the good of the people.

"Deciding whether or not to choose a new name is more difficult than I expected. I have carefully studied many names that might fit parts of my vision, but not all. There were twists and turns I must still study. I need much more time to understand all my vision has to tell me. Until I fully understand, I cannot choose wisely. I will keep my name, at least for now. Perhaps a name will reveal itself later. I have lived with the name, Mawatani, almost all my life, and have been through much. It has served me well. It is who I am. To me, my name is not important. Who I am and intend to be is where I must put my focus. I will keep my name."

The women trilled and the men cried out in celebration.

Many people approached Mawatani, offering encouragement. Little by little, families began to return to their homes. Mawatani and Zicahota remained behind with his cousins and friends, including Matoska. As they were talking, Talks With Owls approached and placed his hand on Mawatani's shoulder.

"You did well, Mawatani. Our people have much to look forward to as you grow and mature. You and I will spend many good hours together."

Mawatani thanked him, and the old man walked away.

By now, Mawatani was exhausted. One night's sleep was not enough to make up for the grueling five days before. He excused himself and headed for his lodge with Zicahota.

Before they entered, Zicahota stopped and put his arm on Mawatani's. "Kola, these days with you have taught me much. I have learned things that will help me in my quest, but even beyond that. Since we met, you have taught me new ways to think. I will never look at a creek or river the same way. Before, I would watch it flow and see its power. I would understand that it was Takuskanskan who caused the water to flow, but I did not relate it to how we live our lives, or how much we can learn from it. It has changed the way I think about everything. It has changed my life. I am grateful you asked me to be part of these important days in your life."

"I'm thankful I did too," Mawatani replied. "You have been a steady rock for me, Zicahota. I will forever be thankful for our friendship. I will try to be as steady for you in your quest."

Looking up, he prayed. "Tunkasila, be with us as we grow into manhood and our futures together. Help us to help our people."

The two boys smiled and turned toward the lodge.

It was a good day.

Glossary

NOTE: Most Lakota words are accented on the second syllable
        Most Cs are pronounced with a ch sound
        Many Ss are pronounced with a sh sound

agli (aglee)......................................they come

agli wanyanka (aglee Wyahnka).......they have returned

amape yanka (amapeh Wyahnka)......wait for me

anpetu wi (anpetu wee)....................the sun

anpo wicahpi (anpo weechahkpee)....the morning star/dawn

Arikara (Arikara)............................a Caddoan tribe

ate' (ateh).....................................father/uncle

ate' mi tawa (ateh me tawa)............. my Father

cansasa chanshasha)......................dried willow bark

canhanpi (chahanpee).....................sugar

cannunpa (channunpa).....................sacred center pole
of sun dance lodge

Cankpe Opa Wakpala (Chahnkpeh
Opee Wahkpahla...........................Wounded Knee Creek

cehinka tapte (cheyheenka tapteh.....full grown cow

four-legged people...........................mammals, rodents, etc.

hanbleceya (hahnblehciya............... vision quest

hanhepi (hanhepee).........................night

hanhepi wi (hahnhepee wee)............moon/night sun

hansni (hanshnee)...........................absolutely no!

Hau (how)......................................hello/good/yes

Hau Ate' (how ateh).........................(in this usage) an
acknowledgement
to Wakan Tanka,
the Great Spirit

hechetu yelo (hechetu yelo).............. that is the way

hehaka (Hayhahka...........................male elk

he wocekiye (hay wochekiyeh...........prayer mountain

heyoka (hayoka)................................	a man who lives backwards-says yes for no; washes with dirt, dries with water: rides horse facing the rear.
hiyuciciya (hayuchichiyah................	handing one his own
hi yanka yo (he yonka yo)................	hold on!/wait
hokahe (hokahay)...........................	signal for action (such as Charge!)
hoksila (hoksheela..........................	child or young boy
hoksila wakan (hoksheela Wakahn....	holy boy
igluhomni (eegluhomnee).................	to turn oneself around/ changing one's behavior
ini (inee).......................................	spiritual steam from sweat bath
ina (eena)......................................	sweat bath
inipi (ineepee)................................	spiritual sweat bath
initi (initee)...................................	sweat-house/lodge
kinnickinnick..................................	used in pipe...made from tobacco.bearberries, sweetgrass, etc.
kola (kola).....................................	friend
koskolaka (koshkolaka)....................	older boy/young man
kte sni (kteh shnee).........................	I will not
kupelo (kupelo)..............................	they come
lakotopiyapi (lakotopeeyapee)..........	medicines from nature
Land of Many Lodges......................	place of real life after death
kte sni (kteh shnee).........................	I will not
kupelo (kupelo)..............................	they come
lakotopiyapi (lakotopeeyapee)..........	medicines from nature
Land of Many Lodges......................	place of real life after death
Makosica (Makosheecha)..................	The Badlands
Miniconjous (Miniconjoo).................	another branch of the Lakota
misunkala (meeisunkala)..................	little brother
Napasni (Napahshnee).....................	strong/brave

Niye kici wawaglaka wacin ye
(Neeyay kichi <u>wo</u>waglaka
wac<u>heen</u> yay.....................................I wish to speak to you

okile (Okeelay)...............................to search for one's own

oniyan (o<u>nee</u>yan)............................breath

otankaya toyola (otankaya toy<u>o</u>la).....extended green; prairie

oyate (oy<u>a</u>teh)...............................a people, nation, tribe

pa (pa<u>ha</u>)......................................mountain

Paha Sapa (Pa<u>ha</u> Sapa.....................Black Hills

parfleche (<u>par</u>flesh)..........................rawhide pouch used
for storing & carrying

peji wacaga kicison (peshi
wa<u>hahn</u>ga kich<u>ee</u>sion........................braid of sweetgrass

peta owihankesni
o<u>wee</u>han<u>keshn</u>ee)......................fire of no end-fireplace
outside sweat lodge
to heat stones

pemmican...buffalo meat, dried &
pounded into a powder;
mixed with cherries
(or other small fruit
and buffalo fat.

pilamaya (peei<u>la</u>maya)......................thank you

pte cincala (pteh chin<u>chala</u>)..............buffalo calf

pte owicile (<u>Pteh</u> ...o<u>wee</u>chilay).........she is looking for her calf

sakehanska (shah<u>ke</u>hanska)..............grizzly bear

sunkawakan (shunka<u>wah</u>kahn...........horse

sunkawakan (shunkawah<u>kahn</u>.........I will give you a horse

sunkmanitu (shung<u>amani</u>too)...........wolf

Takuskanskan (Dakushkanskan)........the spirit of motion

tatanka (ta<u>tahn</u>ka)...........................buffalo

Tatanka Pte Ska (Ta<u>tan</u>ka Pteh Ska)....White Buffalo Woman

tiyospaye (tee<u>yosh</u>pyea)....................tight knit family
community

temni (temnee)..............................sweat

tokola...a policing group
to keep order

toksa (toksha)................................soon

towakan...a person's spirit

travois (travwah)...........................carrier made from
two poles fastened
to horse or dog

Tunkasila (Tunkashila).....................Creator/Grandfather

two-leggeds...................................humans

unci (unchee)..............................grandmother

unpa...to smoke the pipe

uwa yo (uwah yo)...........................come

wacinko (wachinko..........................one who feels
sorry for oneself

wacin ksapa yo...(wachin ksapa yo)...be attentive

wacintanka yo (wacheentanka yo).....be patient with me

wahosi (wahosee)...........................messenger

wahoye (wahhoyeh)........................I promise

wakan (wakahn)............................holy

Wakan Tanka (Wakahn Tanka)..........The Great Mystery
Power/ The Great
Spirit/creator

wakan econpi.................................what we do (spiritually)

wakan iya.....................................what we say
(spiritually)

wakan lowanpi...............................what we sing
(spiritually)

Wakanpi (wakahnpee)......................the spirits (all things
above the people)

Wakinyan (wakinyan).......................Thunderbeings

wakuyeloI have returned to you

wanapnkyo....................................look there

wanbli wapiya (Wanblee Wahpeea)....medicine man who's
healing comes
from the eagle

wan he (wahn hay)..........................look there

waniya (waneeya)...........................human life

wanma yanka yo.............................look at me

wahoye (wahoyeh)..........................I promise

Wanmayankoyo (wahnmayankoyo.....look at me

waun (waoon).....................................I am coming

wicasa wakan (wicasa wahkan).........wise/holy man

winged people...................................birds

Wiwanyan Wacipi (wi<u>wanya</u>n
wacheepee)......................................sun dance